AND FOR YOU

# And for Your Children

*Leading Children Into the*
*Gifts and Fruit of the Spirit*

**CHRIS AND JOHN LEACH**

MONARCH
Crowborough

**British Library Cataloguing in Publication Data**
A catalogue record for this book is available
from the British Library.

ISBN: 1 85424 249 0

Produced by Bookprint Creative Services
P.O. Box 827, BN21 3YJ, England for
MONARCH PUBLICATIONS
Broadway House, The Broadway, Crowborough
East Sussex, TN6 1HQ.
Printed in Great Britain

To our children
Steve and Paul
the greatest teachers we've
ever had

# CONTENTS

Repent and be baptised, every one of you,
in the name of Jesus Christ for the forgiveness of your
sins. And you will receive the gift of the Holy Spirit.
The promise is for you . . .

**And for Your Children**

(Acts 2: 38-39)

# PREFACE

*by the Bishop of Coventry*

John and Chris Leach have made a lively and much appreciated contribution to spiritual renewal and mission in the Diocese of Coventry, and many of us have enjoyed them and their delightful family.

It is good that this book gives an opportunity for John and Chris to contribute to the witness of Christians over a wider area and to help and encourage us all with one of the most vital parts of that witness, our ministry to our own children and our family life. This could be a key Christian contribution to our society at present and the way in which we could most obviously communicate the heart of the Gospel. I hope this book will be widely used.

# ACKNOWLEDGEMENTS

This seems to be a book whose time has come. For several years people have been urging Chris to write up for a wider audience some of the insights she has gained through working with children. She has never had the slightest inclination to do so, nor the least desire to be an author. But one day, out of the blue, after yet another urging by someone to put inkjet to paper, she was filled with a sudden and all-consuming enthusiasm for the project. That night she lay awake planning the outline, within a few weeks a synopsis had been sent off, and a short time later it was all systems go. You now have the finished result.

So we would both like to say a very big thank you to all those who have nagged her for years with no result. Thank you for your faith in her, your appreciation of her ministry to children, and your belief that others could benefit from her expertise. There are too many of you to name, except for one, Mike Lewis, who nagged longest and hardest. We hope you're now happy to see the fruit of your persistence, and that you may, as a side-effect, have learnt something valuable about prayer, which often seems to work in a similar way!

We would also like to thank Peter Lawrence. He only nagged once, as far as we can remember, but in the strange way of things his was the nag which broke the camel's back and set the whole thing in motion.

Then there were those who worked with Chris, and were around while the lessons which this book seeks to share were learnt. Again, there are several of you, but perhaps we might single out Di Marples, a trusty lieutenant for several years who caught the vision, helped it grow and develop, and took up the baton when we moved to Coventry.

We need to record also our tremendous gratitude to Sylvia Figures. As an honorary grandma to Steve and Paul and a wise and loving friend to us she contributed much not just to this book but also to our family. Without her help Chris simply wouldn't have had the time to lead children's ministry, or the encouragement to keep going.

Finally, we need to record our thanks to many others who have contributed (some even deliberately) to this book. From our early years there were those who taught and nurtured us as young Christians, and special appreciation is due to the church family at St Luke's, Cranham Park, where Chris found a spiritual home during her childhood and which I joined much later. It was there that Barry Kissell, without realising it, set in motion a whole train of thought for us about children and parenting, long before we were even married, and this book owes much to him for his inspiration. Some nationally-famous leaders like Ishmael have inspired and encouraged us, and many children from our three parishes have been guinea-pigs as we've learnt the things this book contains.

Then there are those from all sorts of churches with whom we have discussed principles and practice, and among whom we have been allowed to teach and experiment: special thanks must go to Dave and Jan Butler and others from Coventry Christian Fellowship, and Roger Jones and the East Birmingham Renewal Group. And then, of course, there is the whole church family at St James', Styvechale (by the way, it's pronounced Sty-chull) who have shared in our journey and enjoyed with us some of its discoveries. David Green has been singled out for special mention because he helped me to put new guts into my computer, and was always there at the end of the phone when they went wrong (not to mention Sally his wife who always let him drop everything and come round to solve the latest silicon crisis). All these deserve our thanks for what they've given to us, in so many different ways.

But it is our own boys, who provided the impetus to learn and many valuable insights along the way, who deserve the greatest thanks. To them this book is dedicated: they're not perfect, but they love the Lord Jesus and are seeking to live for him.   What more could any parents ask?

But last of all we need to give thanks, and any glory which may be floating around, to the God who sends his Holy Spirit to us and to our children as we seek to live for him and introduce others to him. Our prayer is that this book will help us all experience more of what the Spirit brings.

John Leach

# INTRODUCTION

In several ways this book is about partnership. First it was written by a partnership of two people. John is an Anglican vicar, and is a bit of an author, having published a book on worship called *Liturgy and Liberty* which you might have seen.[1] You might even have read it. He doesn't know all that much about children, but he's good at operating the computer, has a natty turn of phrase on a good day, and was once described by a friend as a 'part-time theologian'.

I, Chris am married to him (John, that is, not the friend), and in each of the three parishes in which we've worked (rural Norfolk, inner-city Sheffield and suburban Coventry) I have led the children's ministry in the church, although it has to be said that my word-processing skills leave a little bit to be desired. So between the two of us we hope we've managed to come up with a reasonable book; rooted in real life, thought-out theologically, and beautifully typed.

Secondly, we want the book to be a partnership between 'How?' and 'Why?', probably because this reflects our own different interests. Mainly, of course, it's about 'How?', because there is not much on the market to tell leaders how children can be helped into fully charismatic Christianity, but the 'Why?' comes in to help us understand at a slightly deeper level what is going on with the children in our care. In terms of its structure, most of the 'Why?' comes in the first four chapters, which look at the place of children with respect to the kingdom of God, their families, their parents and the Christian life. Some books tell you that you can skip the theoretical bits and move straight to the practical chapters if you like: well, you could with this book, but you'd get a lot less out of it, since you wouldn't understand either the nature of the overall task or some of the practicalities along the way.

Next, we wanted the book to reflect the partnership which exists between the gifts and the fruit of the Spirit. Different bits of the church have emphasised each of these two elements: the charismatics have been renowned (not totally unfairly) for their interest in the spectacular and supernatural gifts, while the evangelicals have concentrated much more on the work of the Spirit in the long, slow process of building Christian character into Jesus' followers. As is so often the case in this kind of controversy, both sides are right in what they emphasise and wrong in what they neglect.

So this book will contain material on how to get children prophesying, but it'll also talk about discipline, maturity and all the other work of the Spirit which is seldom sensational but always essential. Being able to speak in tongues and all that does not of itself mean that you are in a right relationship with God, or that your lifestyle accurately reflects biblical standards, as any old Corinthian would be able to tell you. To write a book on how to get children behaving like charismatics would be a relatively easy task, and it would have a certain shock-value to the Christian public, but it might not end up being all that glorifying to God. He really isn't concerned with getting lots of little charismatics anywhere near as much as he is concerned with getting lots of little disciples, and it is the job of parents, children's workers and the Holy Spirit together to make sure he gets as many as he can. So the early chapters are vital if we are to see the bigger picture, and to put the gifts of the Spirit in their rightful place as a part of discipleship and sanctification and not a substitute for it.

Our conviction, though, is that the relationship of gifts and fruit really is a partnership. They come together. You don't see a tree *trying* to have apples, straining and groaning in the way some Christians *try* to become holy. Most trees just seem to stand there, being trees, until one day, quite naturally, little apples begin to appear. What causes this is not effort: it's sap. The roots go deep down and goodness passes up through the inside of the tree, flowing through every part of it, and only emerging to public view in the form of fruit in due season.

This is a helpful picture of the work of the Spirit. Some

Christians rightly stress the importance of fruit, but don't realise that it won't grow if the Spirit is not allowed to flow throughout the life of the believer. Seeking fruit and trying hard to grow it is to miss the point: rather we should seek the life of the Spirit within us, and give him full reign to flow through us. As he does so, he brings gifts. They may be sudden and spectacular, and they may get a lot of attention. They're not fruit, which grows much more slowly, but they can help it to grow. Christians who want to clamp down and restrict the supernatural work of the Spirit may not realise that they can be cutting off the very flow of the Spirit which will nourish and grow the fruit they are seeking. So this book is designed to help us lead our children into both sides of the partnership between fruit and gifts of the Spirit.

Another area of partnership is between the Bible and the Spirit. We are committed to a belief in the authority of the Bible for the church, and also to an awareness of the need for the Holy Spirit to bring it alive. This leads us to yet another partnership, that between knowledge and experience. Generations of children were brought up to know about God through Bible stories, but never taught how to experience his touch on their lives. We'll be arguing, at least to those of you who don't skip the early chapters, that there is more than ever the need for this dimension of Christianity to be rediscovered, especially among youngsters.

So that's a little of what lies in store for you as you begin this book. We hope you'll enjoy it, and we even dare to believe that the Holy Spirit may work in partnership with what we've written to teach and empower you as you lead children into more of his fullness.

**Notes**

1.  John Leach, *Liturgy and Liberty* (MARC: Eastbourne, 1989).

# CHAPTER ONE

# CHILDREN IN THE KINGDOM?

A commonly heard statement is that 'children are the church of tomorrow'. While this is usually supposed to be well-meaning, when you stop and think about it, it's actually demeaning. It implies that they are not *yet* members of the church, but that if we play our cards right they might end up being members. Just what is the place of children with regard to the church and to the kingdom? Are they 'in' or 'out', and on what criteria do we decide?

The answer is that it depends, or appears to depend, on what brand of Christian you ask. In particular you may get three different answers from those who adhere to three different positions, which for the sake of simplicity we will call the 'Baptist', the 'New Church' and the 'Anglican'. While not every Baptist would be a fully signed-up follower of the particular understanding we shall call 'Baptist', and neither would all Anglicans or New Church members of theirs, the praxis and liturgy of these three streams does betray a certain theological position, even if not everyone has fully thought it out. We shall therefore keep the terms safely in inverted commas when they refer to each position.

In the Baptist denomination, children tend to be treated as though they were outside the kingdom and need to be won into it. The normal route to membership is via believers' baptism, which rarely happens before teenage years at the earliest. This sacrament can only rightly be administered to those who have made a conscious 'adult' declaration of faith, with a certain degree of understanding of what they have committed themselves to. Children are 'dedicated' at birth, but this is not generally thought to include them as church members. Rather it expresses the hope that the child will grow into faith in the future, and not an understanding that in some way it already has faith. The hope is that it will grow up and 'become a Christian' such that it can undergo baptism as an adult and subsequently be received into membership, although it may, paradoxically, be allowed to take communion before baptism and membership if it is judged to have had a saving experience of Christ. The job of the parents in all this is therefore to bring up the child so that it will one day want to opt in: in other words they have an *evangelistic* task.

On the other hand, those churches which hold the 'Anglican' view and are happy to practise infant baptism have a different understanding. Children are basically included rather than excluded, and the prayer and desire of the church is not that they'll one day opt in, but rather that they won't one day opt out. This inclusive approach means that the job of parents is much more about *nurturing* and *discipling* than evangelising. A conversion experience is not seen as essential if the child's parents are actively training him or her up in the ways of the Lord (although the move from family faith to personal faith does need to be made in later years). A picture which is often used to explain this is that of the Israelites crossing the Red Sea. No doubt there were among their number on that day children of all ages as well as adults. Some would have toddled through the gap in the waters, some would have been carried in their parents' arms, and some, no doubt, would have slept peacefully through the whole thing, blissfully unaware of the momentous event which God was causing to happen for them. Yet all would have been 'saved' as they reached dry land on the other side, free of the Egyptian threat. To suggest that they were not really saved unless they consciously went through a repeat performance would simply not be true, although it would presumably be possible for them at any stage to get into a boat, cross back the other way, and hand themselves back into slavery. Thus, the argument goes, those children whose parents have 'carried' them into the kingdom and who are helping them to live out that life of freedom, do not need saving again; they need help and encouragement to live life to the full in the promised land.

The New Churches are much harder to get hold of doctrinally, since the term refers to a network rather than to an organisation with set doctrines and practices. But the general understanding seems to be somewhere between the two already mentioned. As far as it is possible to lump them all together, the New Churches have a theology which looks Anglican in all but infant baptism. Children are included in the kingdom – in fact Jesus said they were a paradigm of it – but they do need to be led into the fullness of their inheritance. They will be valued in the church and encouraged to move in ministry and in spiritual gifts, and may be allowed to receive the bread and wine at communion, but can't be baptised until they're 'adults'. They're not treated as if they were little heathens in need of evangelising, but at the same time they are not seen as fully-integrated members of the church.

This may look pretty similar in some ways to the 'Anglican' position, but the New Churches don't usually go the whole hog with Anglicanism by granting children the sacramental sign of the membership they supposedly have, and will administer baptism only to 'adults'.[1] (It is usually the case that infant baptism is not recognised in the New Churches, and adults who join after an Anglican 'sprinkling' as babies will be urged to undergo a 'proper' baptism by immersion.)

Thus the role of parents is slightly less simple than for Anglican or Baptist parents: it is usually seen in terms of encouraging children to 'grow into their inheritance'. It's not evangelistic, since the children already have some relationship with God, but it is not totally nurturing either, because there is a sense in which they are still only 'potential' members of the kingdom rather than fully sacramentally-integrated ones.

No doubt there are other shades of grey in between the black-and-white alternatives of evangelising non-Christians and discipling Christians, and you and your church will have your own understanding of the theology of children and the kingdom (at least you should have!). But all this so far implies that the children in question are those of Christian parents, and are being brought up in an environment of faith and nurture. What of the vast majority of children in our world who have no such background?

Surely the New-Church idea of 'inheritance' is helpful here. If we take at face value Jesus' words in Matthew 18:1-9 and 19:13-15, we must believe three things: that the kingdom belongs to children; that if someone loses their child-like innocence and humility they are in danger of losing the kingdom too, and that it is possible for people to come between children and their place in the kingdom. We have to be child-like to enter the kingdom, and while children seem to be good at this naturally, the adults to whom Jesus was speaking had specifically to change. To take on this humility would lead an individual to greatness in the kingdom, but to refuse to do so would put him in danger both of his own eternal life and also possibly of leading others astray from gaining theirs.

If, then, children by their very nature are those already included in the kingdom, they can grow up in one of three ways. First, they may be taught to grow and value the things of God, and they may remain within his purposes and mature into adult believers. Secondly, they may be brought up in an environment of faith but later harden themselves and opt out. Or thirdly, they may grow up completely ignorant of the inheritance they have because neither their parents nor anyone else close to them has ever told them about it. This would be the state of children of no Christian background, and many of them would and do lose out on their inheritance simply through ignorance and by default.

This begs another important question: at what age do they pass from being 'children' to 'adults'? If children lose their relationship with God either through ignorance or by deliberate choice, at what stage can this be said to happen? There was much debate in the past in Baptist circles about the 'age of understanding' after which children would be consigned to the fires of hell if they hadn't got their act together with God. Nobody was able to say what this age was, but many children, like John, grew up in terror of reaching it!

The obvious answer to this question is that there is no answer. Children vary tremendously in their development physically, intellectually and emotionally, so why should their spiritual development be any less undefined? Some, however, would want to see pointers here in the Jewish ceremony of *Bar-Mitzvah*, which was supposed to mark this transition liturgically as a distinct rite-of-passage at about the age of twelve. Some also feel that Luke's account of Jesus' trip to the Temple at the age of twelve similarly points to somewhere around that age as an important spiritual transition point, and our experience of having had one son make the transition to secondary school at eleven would make us want to agree broadly with this sort of age as a significant change point.

But in terms of young children without Christian nurture or background in the home, we would want to say that they belong to

God but have never been told so. Our work as churches with such 'unchurched' children is not to evangelise them in the sense of calling them to repent or fear the eternal frying pan, but rather to tell them the good news that they are already saved, and help them to get to know the friend and Lord who has them in his loving care.

So can we summarise our understanding of the place of children before God, and is there anything we can do to reconcile these differing positions? First of all, very few Christians would want to deny the *possibility* of children having an experience, even a saving experience, of Christ at an early age, whether before or after baptism. Whether or not this is expected to be the norm, it seems clear that it can happen, and all would hope that it would happen. Secondly, it may be less helpful to draw a great distinction between the two extremes of evangelising and discipling, and more appropriate to think in terms of leading children on in faith, whether this is seen to be before or after conversion. The 'inheritance' language of the New Churches is again helpful here. And while we'll go on to argue that this leading on is best done by parents within a family, there will be many children who will need to have surrogate spiritual families in order that they become aware of God and his place in their lives.

In terms of our own position, and the viewpoint from which this book will be written, we'd better come clean and own up to being thoroughly convinced Anglicans. We believe that children are included in the kingdom by default, and that if their parents or others close to them are actively wanting, hoping and praying for them to be, they can be included in a covenant relationship with God in which they are helped to grow to adult maturity. As Anglicans we are happy that such children are baptised,[2] since there seems little point in refusing to allow children the initiation ceremony into something to which we believe they already belong. ('You can be a Brownie, come to meetings, join in the games, take badges and come on camps, but you can't jump over the toadstool until you're grown up').[3] Children of Christian parents have a relationship with Jesus already, and they have it because their parents are giving it to them. Children of non-Christian parents also have a relationship with Jesus, which they don't know about yet. We see the job of children's ministry in a church, therefore, being to back up the parents' work by encouraging the children to grow in this relationship, or to give children the information they're not getting from parents. They may, of course, subsequently opt out of living the Christian life, in which case their baptism won't be of much help to them. The fact that you once jumped over a toadstool is worth very little if you have ceased to live as a Brownie or believe in the principles of Browniehood (or should it be Brownieship?).

So we are Anglican, and so will this book be, but we hope you'll forgive us for that if necessary, and allow this book to help and encourage you anyway!

In the next chapter we'll move on to a subject in some ways less controversial, but in others more: what does God expect of children, and how can families help?

### Notes

1. The term 'adult' used in this way is not really an indication of a particular age (policies over which may vary considerably in different churches) but is simply opposed to the term 'infant', meaning a very young child or baby who cannot possibly have any intellectual grasp of the faith.
2. The whole question of infant baptism policy in the Anglican Church is a minefield, and it is perhaps due to the pastoral mess we've made of it that other churches like the New Churches won't touch it with a bargepole. Nevertheless, we feel that the theology stands, and the pastoral practice needs to be brought into line. See Colin Buchanan, *Infant Baptism and the Gospel* (DLT: London, 1993).
3. Or whatever it is they do. Having only boys, we're not certain!

# CHAPTER TWO

# CHILDREN IN FAMILIES

We've looked at the place of children theologically, and now we must move on to ask where they fit sociologically. Although this book is about the role of the church in leading children on in spirituality, we can't ignore the fact that their primary setting is not church but family. This chapter will explore the state of play with regard to family life at the end of the twentieth century, and we'll attempt a bit of part-time theologising about family life.

The picture conjured up by the word 'family' would vary considerably depending on when and where you heard it. If you were an ancient Israelite you would think immediately in terms of what we would now call 'tribe' – a collection of people related through common ancestry, some of whom might be around now but many of whom would have died long hence. If you lived at about the time of Jesus you'd think in pretty much the same terms, but with perhaps more emphasis on those whom you actually related to now because they lived with or near you. If you were an English Victorian living at the end of the last century you'd probably think about what we now call the 'extended family' – various aunts, uncles and grandparents who shared a house or at least a street with you. As this century has progressed, the term 'family' would increasingly have painted for you a picture of a mum, a dad and 2·4 children living in a little box somewhere, and as the century draws to its close even this small unit would be replaced with various models involving only one parent, or even 'alternatives' such as a homosexual couple with or without children. What has happened, particularly in this century, is that 'family' has become increasingly fragmented into smaller and smaller units, such that some prophets fear a return to an epidemic of orphanage, where neither couple in a relationship want responsibility for the children they have created.

These sociological trends hide some disturbing facts. There surely must be a relationship between the breakdown of stable family life and the increasing crime rate, particularly among juveniles, the murder of millions of foetuses through abortion, the spread of sexually-transmitted diseases (and now of course AIDS), the impermanence of marriage and the increase in uncommitted cohabitation, and many other terrifying trends in our society.

The question to ask with regard to all this is surely, 'How can we do "family" properly?' We're not convinced, at least if we take the Bible at all seriously, that all this living together and gay business is really what God wants for us, and we can see all too clearly where it's all heading. Many of us feel the need to go back somehow to where we went wrong and make a stand for something better, but to where exactly do we go back? Those of us living in this time of single parenting wish we could get back to stable nuclear families, but older people can see the incredible pressures put on parents by the loss of the extended family and the expectation that two parents should now fulfil all the roles previously covered by a multitude of more distant relatives. They'd want to go back even further. And so it goes on. Where do we look for a 'real' model of family life?

In some areas the church is doing much to supplement the work of the fast-disintegrating nuclear family. Many local churches consciously refer to themselves as 'The Church Family', and go to great pains to assure everyone (especially the elderly or single) that their 'Family Service' isn't just for Mum, Dad and kids but is for the family of the church. They enjoy 'Family' social events, and make a great song and dance (at least if they are Anglicans) about 'The Peace' – that anything-but-peaceful part of the service where everyone cuddles everyone else. If you want to measure the extent to which a church has gone down this family track, take a stop-watch and time this all-in extravaganza. The longer it goes on for, the more people see themselves as belonging to a family: this is a complete contrast to the Eight o'Clock Communion mentality where the idea is to avoid others, not to hug them!

But some see dangers in this. 'If you have [a family] model of the church,' says the Dean of Bristol Cathedral, arguing strongly that to do so is a grave mistake, 'then ministry tends to become parental.' Not necessarily, he reassures us, by people expecting to be called 'Father'. Instead, 'the role that the ministers have becomes like that of parents. In other words, they become those who are looked to for guidance.'[1] Leaving aside the questions of why the term 'parental' should be used, as it was throughout Dr Carr's talk, as a pejorative term, and why church leaders shouldn't be looked to for guidance, there is clearly a big question mark over whether it is the job of church to be or even look like a family, substituting for something which the sociologists would more easily recognise as such. Isn't church just different, and shouldn't it stick to being church?

On one occasion Jesus faced this same question, although it wasn't exactly posed as a question. In Matthew chapter 12 we read of the incident where he was preaching and was sought out by his nuclear (and incidentally single-parent) family. His reply in verse 48 raises the question as to what exactly 'family' means, and his answer is that actually his real family consists of those who are obedient to him and living in the kingdom, that is the church. He re-emphasises this in chapter 19, where he promises that those who have left behind human families in order to be active in the kingdom will be rewarded many times over with replacement family members galore. So what is Jesus actually saying here?

Surely his point is that rather than trying to read family back into church, we should read church forward into family? God's original purpose that we should not be alone was intended to be fulfilled by his placing us in horizontal relationships with other humans under a vertical relationship with him, and he created the church to be the context for these relationships. In other words, God's people should be what we call 'brothers' and 'sisters' under a loving 'father'. If you want to know what a family really is, says Jesus, look at the church: not the fallen and divided church you live in at the moment, with its squabbles, power struggles, jumble sales and genteel anarchy, but the ideal church as conceived in the loving heart of our father God. That's the model, and far from it being dangerous when the church begins to look like a family, it is in fact a sign of hope that we are getting closer to being the perfect company of God's people that we were planned to be. If the term 'parental' is seen as a negative term, it is because we have a human rather than a divine model.

This has another great value if we accept it. It can be very tempting for us either to sit in judgement over, or to feel condemned by, others whose family life we perceive to be worse or better than our own. These attitudes can manifest themselves in various ways, from the vociferous condemnation in some evangelical circles of one-parent or gay families, to the sense of being in some way 'second class' which divorced people can feel in some churches, right through to the slight sense of guilt some of us felt when some really switched-on parishes began to experiment with community and extended families in the seventies. It is easy to see others as either better or worse than ourselves when we judge by human standards. But if we accept that the perfect family is the community of God's people, it follows that every single one of us lives in a dysfunctional family which has been fragmented by sin and division. There's no room for name-calling or inferiority, because even the healthiest of us is still in a desperate state in comparison with God's perfect will for us. Close up, a Volvo Estate may look far superior to a Fiat 850, but if you look down on them from the top of the Eiffel Tower, they both look pretty insubstantial. Our job is surely to work towards the perfection of God, no matter where we're starting from.

Now of course we can't escape from our culture and sociology, but there is much we can do within it. Most of us are stuck in nuclear families, and suddenly deciding that really our family is the church universal doesn't actually help much. But what we can do is to go about the business of building, wherever we are, little communities which reflect as accurately as they can the big community of which we are a part under God. Our families, whatever their size, and our churches (and their subdivisions – for example, homegroups) should be growing towards the family likeness of the family of God throughout space and time.

This sets up a complex and paradoxical set of relationships, but it is so important to understand them that we need to mention them here. In fact a misunderstanding of them can lead to all sorts of very common disasters. We are living in the overlap between two worlds, or rather, to stay with the analogy, two families. First of all we live in human families, which have human fathers, mothers and children, as well as more distant relatives. But secondly we are living in the universal family of God, his church. This means that our role, and especially our role as parents, will vary from time to time depending on which family we're thinking of.

To take a couple of examples, John is a father to Steve and Paul, and as such rightly has authority over them: they are in a vertical relationship, or a hierarchy. But if the focus is switched to the family of God, the relationships change: John, Steve and Paul are all brothers together under the fatherhood of God. Both these things are true, and at different times it will be appropriate to live one or other of them out. Practically it will mean that at times John as father will discipline and expect apologies from the boys, and will require at times that they apologise to one another. But at other times John as brother may need to apologise to the boys because he has treated them in a way with which father God is not pleased. This is a very commonly-neglected idea: parents expect to hear 'sorry' from their children, but are seldom prepared to say it to them.

Another example of the same thing is the Bible's apparent ambivalence on the issue of men, women and headship. The New Testament can say at one moment that a man has headship over a woman, and then at another that there is in Christ neither male nor female, but oneness. Again, it depends what your context is, and we've so often misunderstood this. Chris as 'wife' is perfectly happy to see herself as being under the 'headship' of John, and finds great security in knowing that the buck ultimately stops with her husband. She even promised that she would obey him, a very unfashionable thing even sixteen years ago! But Chris as 'sister' of John under the headship of God our father is in an exactly equal relationship, and both of us will need at times to submit to one another out of reverence to Christ.

So there is more to families than just a hierarchical relationship, and Christians ignore or misunderstand this at their peril. Nevertheless, there is one important requirement for families, or rather particularly for children within them. To this we shall now move, and we shall look at it carefully since we believe it is vitally important for the correct functioning of both church and society. Because of this it is under severe and sustained attack by the Enemy, who has gained much ground through his lies in this area.

We had planned to start 1994 at our church with a teaching series on 'The Family' (interestingly, John had decided this a couple of months previously, and had then found out the very next day that 1994 was to be 'The Year of the Family', although he never did find out who said so). So some preparatory Bible study began. The discoveries John made became highly important to our church and to us as a family, and they have a bearing on what we're trying to say here.

The first question was to ask of the Bible, 'What has God got to say to parents?', and there is no shortage of answers. There are many passages in Deuteronomy about the need to *teach* their children the ways of God,[2] several in Proverbs about the need to *train* and *correct* them,[3] an admonition from St Paul about the need to *provide* for them,[4] and last but not least the famous 'household codes' in Ephesians and Colossians where fathers are told not to exasperate or embitter their children.[5] And of course the whole implicit context for all this is one of self-giving, committed love. Christian parenting is quite a job, in case you hadn't noticed, and the Bible has lots to say on the subject.

But about the second question, 'What does God want from children?', there is not the same vast quantity of information. In fact, no matter how hard we tried, we could find only one command to children in the whole Bible. We'd thought maybe God wanted children to love him, worship him, read the Bible, not torture their siblings, not get too near the cat with Dad's chainsaw; but none of these featured at all. He might well want these particular things, but the Bible doesn't say so explicitly. Instead there is one command to children and one only: they should obey their parents.

This is most clearly stated in the household codes mentioned above,[6] but is implicit in much of the teaching to youngsters in the Wisdom literature.[7] It may even be one of the Ten Commandments, depending on how you interpret Exodus 20:12. The primary meaning is more probably about respecting and caring for parents in their old age, (rather than writing them off and marginalising them, which is the way our society often deals with them), and as such this commandment is not really addressed to the very young, but the author of Ephesians clearly feels able to reinterpret the text to refer to children, since he uses it as a proof text to back up his command to obey parents. So this wealth of material for parents, contrasted with the single solitary command to children, led us to an important conclusion: obedience matters, and it matters early.

Of course, the obedience needs to come out of respect rather than fear, and God has built in a safety device for this. That's why he has so much to say to parents. If obeyed, the instructions to them which we've already mentioned would ensure that cruelty and fear had no place at all in family life. And of course, God wants grown-ups themselves to be obedient too; you can't get very far into the Bible without reaching that conclusion. So the whole context is one of loving relationships on human and divine levels.

But it does seem that the one vital thing for children to learn, and parents to teach, is the place of obedience. It's almost as if the one fundamental crawl-before-you-walk lesson for children is that obedience counts. If a child learns that lesson thoroughly at home, it's a lesson which will stay with him for life. But if he doesn't, or if he learns that disobedience is really no big deal, severe problems will result.

If obedience really is such a vital issue, the Bible also has much to say about the consequences of ignoring it. If you look at some of the gloom-and-doom passages, it's amazing how often disobedience is featured among the symptoms of a society gone wrong. In Romans chapter 1, Paul describes the slippery slope into depravity which the world has taken since it failed to acknowledge God or thank him, and in there among the idolatry, homosexuality and murder is the comment in verse 30 that people 'disobey their parents'. This sounds a bit limp, and rather an anticlimax after all the more juicy sins around it, until you realise the full implications. The author of the Pastoral Epistles tells his young protégé to watch out for the terrible times of the last days, a feature of which will be disobedience to parents (2 Tim 3:2), and Titus, along with Timothy, is similarly warned not to appoint church leaders whose children could be accused of being 'wild and disobedient', but rather those who can manage their household well, and therefore do the same for the church.[8]

In the Old Testament there is a wonderful passage in Deuteronomy 21:18-21 about the way to treat your rebellious son by getting the elders at the gate of the town to stone him to death for you (we used this as the reading one Mothering Sunday), and the story of Eli's wicked sons, Hophni and Phineas, shows what happens if you don't do this: God does it for you, and then does it to you as well. In 1 Samuel 3:13, Eli and his sons are held accountable, and all three of them end up dead by the end of the next chapter. Stories like these serve to illustrate the importance God places on obedience, even though nowadays we're the other side of *the* death which means that no more blood need be shed for sin.

If rebellion and disobedience to parents are marks of a sick society which has turned its back on God, there is hope. God is calling those who, like Abraham, will direct their children and their households to keep the way of the Lord by doing what is right and just (Gen 18:19), and a mark of the coming of the kingdom of God will be the restoration of family relationships. Malachi 4:6, picked up and quoted by the angel to Zechariah in Luke 1:17, looks forward to the time when the hearts of children will be turned back to their fathers, and obedience will be restored.

It really does seem that obedience is a key issue. Perhaps that is why it is under so much attack, and why the neglect of it can be so ruinous for society. You don't have to look very far in our world to see what little respect there is among the young for their parents or indeed any authority; the rising juvenile crime rate, and the increasing seriousness of that crime; the despair of authorities as to how to staunch it; the rock-bottom morale in education as teachers are sent in each day to face thirty-odd children who simply do not know what obedience means; and perhaps above all the shoulder-shrugging despair of parents, and even Christian parents, who just don't know how to cope with their offspring: all these speak of a society which has forgotten how to discipline. There is, of course, the problem of over-discipline, and children who have been bullied, beaten and abused by raging fathers are in plentiful supply. But this has contributed to the problem via another route and helped to make it axiomatic in liberal circles that children are not to be physically punished at all; there have even been attempts, successful in some areas, to make smacking a criminal offence. The Enemy loves all this: as long as he can get people to leave behind biblical teaching, he's not that fussy about which direction they veer off in. A child who has been beaten up and a child who doesn't know what the word 'no' means are equally delightful to him.

All sorts of ills in society can be traced back to disobedience and family breakdown if you think about it. We used to live in Sheffield, and we can well remember the day when we heard that there had been a disaster at Hillsborough football ground, about two miles from our house, which had claimed nearly a hundred lives. John went down to the mortuary, with other local priests, to try to minister to the relatives coming to identify crushed bodies, and to the staff who had never had to cope with anything like this before, and even to the police, who naturally got the blame for the whole thing. Reflecting on the experience, we thought that something like that just wouldn't have happened when families went to football matches together and therefore youngsters' behaviour was controlled by fathers. Now undisciplined gangs are the normal trouble-makers, behaving as teenagers do when they get together without parental restraint.

Another symptom of the same thing can be seen within the legal system of this country. John regularly has to go to Court (only to lead morning prayers, you'll be relieved to hear), and some of the older staff can see the change in attitude which has taken place. There used to be the old lags who would appear before the magistrates, call them 'Sir' or 'Madam', recognise that it was a fair cop, and say, 'Thank you,' when they were sent down (again). But nowadays the young offenders remain surly, unco-operative and disrespectful. The only crime they'll admit to, it appears, was getting caught. Apparently it is getting harder and harder in some Crown Courts to get a conviction, because the jurors, seeing the poor criminal alone in the dock confronted by the massed authority figures of judge, lawyers and police, immediately side with him as the oppressed underdog. It's like that time when a social worker, refusing like the Priest and the Levite just to pass by on the other side, stopped and looked at the battered and bloodstained body lying in the gutter and said to herself, 'Whoever did this really needs help!'

Of course you can't blame every disaster in society on bad parenting and disobedient children, but perhaps it is a much greater factor in many than would at first appear.

So God demands that children obey and respect their parents, and society suffers when his demands are ignored. But there is an even greater danger, and this we'll move on to deal with in the next chapter.

## Notes

1. Wesley Carr, transcript of a tape at the Coventry Joint Chapters meeting, October 1993.
2. eg, Dt 4:9, 6:7, 6:20, 11:19, 21:19, 31:13.
3. eg, Prov 13:24, 19:18, 22:6, 22:15, 23:13.
4. 2 Cor 12:14.
5. Eph 6:4; Col 3:21.
6. Eph 6:1; Col 3:20.
7. eg, Ps 34:11; Prov 1:8, 6:20, 7:1, 10:1, 23:22; Eccles 12:1.
8. 1 Tim 3:4,5,12; Titus 1:6.

# CHAPTER THREE

# THE ORDINATION OF PARENTS

You can't possibly have failed to notice that in our branch of the church universal there has been quite a bit of arguing recently about whether or not women should or indeed can be ordained to the priesthood. Far be it from us to enter into this argument, which will probably go on for years anyway, but we do want to make a stand for a campaign which has received far less publicity: the ordination of parents. The priesthood of parents is a subject which is vital, but which is often neglected or misunderstood. So what is it, and what should we be doing about it?

The Old Testament priesthood, in common with that of many other religions, had a dual role: the representation of God to people and people to God. Many Old Testament characters, whether or not they were formally and liturgically thought of as priests, fulfilled these tasks. Moses is perhaps a prime example, and he seems to divide his time fairly equally between telling the people what God wants, and telling God what the people want. In other words he has a prophetic and an intercessory role. By the way he fulfils these roles, he reveals something of the nature of God. Samuel was another character who acted both prophetically and in an intercessory role.

When Jesus came, he came with the supreme revelation of God, such that he was able to say to Philip, 'Anyone who has seen me has seen the Father' (Jn 14:9). He came also to pray long and hard for his followers and their ministry: not without cause was he referred to as our Great High Priest. Such was his once-for-all sacrifice of himself, that the human priesthood was no longer needed. People no longer need to gain access to God via a human institution and liturgical sacrifices: now they come into his presence by the shed blood of Jesus and in the power of the Holy Spirit.

And yet . . . in spite of this impeccably sound theology, the fact remains that most of us do actually need a bit of down-to-earth human help. Other people certainly can't win access to God for us, but they can help us to understand that the access has been won by Jesus, and help us to go in. It seems sometimes that the protestant churches, founded quite rightly to stand against the excesses of sacerdotalism before the Reformation, can go too far the other way when they refuse any place at all for 'priestly ministry' in the church. Another baby has gone swirling down the plug-hole, and it is time it was fished out. No man is an island, especially not spiritually, and the fact of the matter is that we learn much of what we know about God via other human beings, and foremost among them are our parents.

It is a truism of psychology that for very young babies, the parents, and especially the mother, are 'God'. They are for a tiny infant the supreme power, the great provider, the one who loves or punishes, who has the ability to give or withhold, to comfort or distress. Babies are totally dependent, and literally owe their life and its continuance to them. They haven't got the intellectual ability to theologise, but they know milk when they taste it, and they also know the lack of it.

As growth and development continues, children begin to be able to differentiate, although it may take years before they become aware of the fact that there is, or might be, a being even more supreme than Mum. And, most important of all, by the time they do realise this, much of their interpretation of that being will have been programmed by the 'God' they've had up until now. In other words, a child's view of God will have been set to a high degree by their parents' revelation of him.

If this sounds far-fetched, ask anyone with experience in Christian counselling about it. They will point you to hundreds of people who have difficulty, for example, with a God who forgives. Why? Because their parents held grudges and continually dredged up past misdemeanours. Or perhaps the difficulty will be over a God who loves unconditionally and unchangingly. Why? Because they grew up with parents who pushed and demanded and gave the impression that only if they achieved would they be loved. The fact is that the way we parent our children puts into them a picture of God which will linger in their emotions and actions long after God himself has been either rejected or embraced. Our parents' generation have left to us a legacy of large numbers of adult Christians unable to relate to the true God because they've been predisposed to recognise only a tawdry substitute. There is plentiful grace for healing, but prevention is better than cure, and the parents of today need to wake up to their priestly role before another generation is crippled.

Now if as parents we reveal 'God' to our children by the way we treat them, for better or worse, we have a vital task but a ridiculously easy way to carry it out. We simply have to treat them, all the time, as we know God would. So when Steve slam-dunks his basketball through the garage window, our immediate and instinctive reaction is to say to ourselves, 'What would God say here?' When Paul plays Lemmings that bit too effectively on the computer and wipes John's five-year preaching plan off the hard disk, it's the same: 'How would God deal with this situation?' Now of course if this is going to work there is one important precondition: we must know God well enough to be able to answer our own questions with a fair degree of accuracy.

In other words what we're saying is that the task of parenting is essentially a *theological* one. Once you realise this, it's the case that the better we know God ourselves, the better we'll be at revealing him to our children. If we get it right, they'll grow up with an inbuilt understanding of what God is like which will resonate with the real thing later rather than drown it out.

Now for something fascinating and terrifying. What exactly is it that God would have us as parents reveal about him? Well, lots of things, obviously. We looked at some of them in the last chapter. That he is a loving God, a provider, a carer and a teacher; that he is faithful and reliable, and so on. Whenever we behave towards our children in these ways, we are revealing the nature of God to them.

But what if we turn the question upside down, and ask not what God wants parents to reveal, but what he wants children to learn? Again, referring back to the last chapter, we said that this way round it was much simpler, and that there was one issue and one alone: *he wants children to know that he is to be obeyed*. This is the absolute nub of the matter, and this is where the Enemy's tactics have most ruined both church and society. We are, quite simply, growing up in a generation which has forgotten how to obey, because it has never been taught, and out of it is coming a church which is the same.

In the last chapter we looked at some of the human and sociological consequences of disobedience, but have you ever stopped to think of the spiritual ones? In a youth group we once ran was a girl whose parents we loved dearly, but who never ever seemed to say 'no' to her or her brother. They had plenty of money in the family, and nothing was too much trouble or too expensive. They were kindly souls, and extremely loving and affectionate in the way they brought up their children. They might get slightly irked with their offsprings' misdemeanours, and on one historic occasion had even been known to shout a bit, but generally speaking they were sweetness and light. It wasn't long before we realised, as her youth group leaders, that their daughter had exactly the same sort of God. She did know right from wrong, but didn't feel at all that it mattered. God might get a bit sad, as her parents might, if she went out and got drunk, or if she slept with her boyfriend, or tried smoking dope once or twice, or anything else really, but it wouldn't spoil the relationship, and he certainly wouldn't get angry, or expect her to stop. In trying to help her growth and discipleship, we realised we were fighting a losing battle, and that the model her parents had shown her had been well and truly transferred onto God: obedience was optional. She had swallowed a huge lie, and we had only to wait for the consequences to be worked out in her spiritual life.

In the same way, many Christians today, who have never been taught that obedience to parents is essential, have no problem with disobeying God. When you look at the flabby, compromised, ineffectual nature of much of the church, it is easy to see the consequences, just as you would if the British Army decided that obeying orders was only necessary for the really keen.

When you look back to the story in Genesis about the fall of mankind, you can see this very issue as the origin of all the evil this world has ever known. God gives clear instructions, but Eve, and then Adam, choose to disobey. The crucial issue here is obedience: they had to learn the hard way that God demands it, and that trouble results if we don't give it. The problems which result are manifold.

Take money, for example. OK, tithing isn't *commanded* in the New Testament, but serious giving is expected, and many Christians have found that the Old Testament teaching still works for them. The Bible's basic assumption is that all we have belongs to God, and that he graciously allows us to keep some to live on ourselves. But now we treat giving rather like our income tax: what's the least possible amount I'm assessable for, and can I get away without giving even that much? The way most of us handle our money is nothing short of downright disobedient, but we don't feel it matters. God'll still be nice to us, just as he will if we carry on being disobedient over what he has told us about stopping gossiping, respect for church leaders, evangelism, and just about everything else we don't fancy thank you very much. And even if we do acknowledge that we might just have a teeny bit of a problem over something like this, the answer is to 'pray it through' or even to 'get some counselling' about it. Anything in fact rather than face the truth that we are arrogant, rebellious and disobedient, and that God is grossly displeased with us. We just do not have in our mindset a view of God which makes us feel that our first duty is to obey him: we'll happily negotiate, but simply to obey is much more theologically difficult.

The consequences of this are only too plain to see. The church is riddled with nominality (which might usefully be defined as Christianity without putting oneself out). It is a byword for bumbling ineffectuality: it faces financial crisis after financial crisis, its leaders fall from grace into immorality, watched by the gloating media, and people in their droves turn to the New Age Movement to find some real spirituality, or to Islam to find some real discipline. Things would be so very different if only we had the kind of respect for God which demanded that we take him seriously.

But hang on: isn't this all a bit severe? Aren't we supposed to *love* God? This line of thinking would make us into people who are terrified of him. It all sounds a bit too 'Old Testament'. Now that Jesus has come to be our friend and brother, do we really need such a harsh God? These are serious objections, and do need to be dealt with. Fortunately it is very easy to do so.

First of all, it's worth mentioning the fact that fear in general has got rather more of a bad name than it perhaps deserves. John is terrified of flashing blue lights when he's going down the M40, so he sticks to seventy mph – just in case (you didn't realise this was a work of fiction, did you?). He also avoids chewing live electric cables, standing on one leg on the edge of cliffs, counselling attractive women alone, and several other things which might otherwise be fun to do. Is he repressed by the tyrant 'fear', and is his freedom impaired? Or does his attitude in fact serve a useful purpose in keeping him alive and out of prison?

So purely on a secular level fear can be useful, but there's a theological dimension too. Whether we like it or not, the 'fear of the Lord' is a concept common to both testaments, and is consistently upheld as something good and right. There are many references to it, which we won't list now since any concordance will do the job for you, but they can perhaps be best summed up in the words of the Preacher as he concludes his philosophical examination of the meaning of life, the universe and everything:

> Now all has been heard;
> here is the conclusion of the matter:
> Fear God and keep his commandments
> for this is the whole duty of man. (Eccl 12:13)

In a New Testament counterpart, Peter tells the would-be disciples to 'live as free men, but do not use your freedom as a cover-up for evil; live as servants of God. Show proper respect to everyone: Love the brotherhood of believers, fear God, honour the king' (1 Pet 2:16-17).

Fearing God is obviously a respectable thing to do, but shouldn't we love God rather than fear him? Well, we need to have a look at what fear actually is, but first we'll note in passing that to Jesus, love and obedience were not opposite options. 'If you love me,' he told his followers, 'you will obey what I command' (Jn 14:15). This is a common theme in the Johannine writings, and is perhaps best expressed in 1 John chapter 2:3-6.

> We know that we have come to know him if we obey his commands. The man who says 'I know him' but does not do what he commands is a liar, and the truth is not in him. But if anyone obeys his word, God's love is truly made complete in

him. This is how we know we are in him: Whoever claims to live in him must walk as Jesus did.

You can't have it much clearer than that!

But let's return for a moment to the human family to see if we can understand the concept of the 'fear of God' any better. When our boys were small, we used to indulge from time to time in that thoroughly biblical practice of smacking. We tried, although not always successfully, to make sure that we never smacked in temper, but rather in a somewhat cold and detached way a short time after the crime had occurred rather than at the time of it. Most times it really did hurt us more than it hurt them, and we were left saddened by their tears. As they grew bigger, they learnt the lesson that naughtiness brought a smack in its wake, providing that it was serious enough to warrant one, and so smacking became something of a deterrent, particularly since we used the highly effective 'three smack' rule, which meant that if they repeated a particular transgression they would get two smacks the next time, and three for a third attempt (we never ever had to administer three). It could be argued, therefore, that they 'feared' us, or rather the punishment we would bring. At times we could see the fear on their faces as they knew they were about to receive physical punishment, and at times we could see them stopping and thinking and deciding not to do something or other because they understood what the consequences would be.

But now they're older. We can't remember the last time we smacked either of them, and we don't feel as if they stalk around in terror lest they meet up with their ultra-violent parents in some dark vicarage corridor; neither (as far as we know) have they ever felt the need to phone Childline because of us. But they do seem to have held on to a sense of fear which is very different from that in their younger days: fear of upsetting or disappointing us. They will still occasionally weep bitter tears after a telling-off, not because their bottoms hurt but because they know our feelings are. Explaining to them how they let themselves and us down, and that we know and they know that they can do better, and so on, has up till now been punishment enough. They wouldn't have understood the subtleties of that approach when they were toddlers, so we used a more direct and physical way of showing our displeasure. But now it isn't necessary, and they fear hurting us more than they fear being hurt by us.

Isn't this the kind of fear the Bible asks of us towards God? Many people have never grown up beyond the stage of fearing that at any minute, and for the slightest peccadillo, God will smite them from on high with illness, redundancy, bereavement or whatever. Either one of these events does occur, in which case they told you so, or it doesn't, which leads inexorably to the conclusion that God's bark is really worse than his bite, and it won't hurt to do just what we want to do. But surely God calls us to grow up into something better? He wants us to have as our deepest fear that we might by our thoughts, words or deeds do something below our status as sons and daughters of the King of kings, something which would bring great displeasure to him, something which would serve to betray the shallowness of our love for him. If we have this kind of fear, we will, in the words of Tate and Brady's hymn, 'Have nothing else to fear.' This is clean fear, holy fear, so unlike the terror of getting beaten up by a violent and capricious God who is simply out to find an excuse to get us. So we give money as Christians, to return to an earlier example, not because we fear God will smite us with a plague of bankruptcy if we don't, but rather because we know his heart well enough to understand how deeply it hurts him to see his bride going about in Oxfam-shop rejects and being mocked by the watching world for her impoverishment. We simply don't want to be a part of anything which causes the Father we love so much pain.

There is one more point, while we are arguing as it were backwards, from man to God, rather than the other way round. It is possible to run human families in such a way that the negative sort of fear never grows into holy fear. We all know of situations where children, even quite old ones, live in terror of some kind of physical abuse from a rage-filled or drunken parent. But God could never be like that because, as we've already seen, there are far more rules for parents than for children. It is quite possible to get children to obey, but to do so while contravening all that the Bible says about the need to nurture and not exasperate them. It really is a two-way thing. Expecting children to obey without expecting parents to love is a recipe for terror; expecting parents to love without expecting children to obey is a recipe for indulgence; but doing both together will lead to godly and obedient children and happy family relationships, and ultimately to a much more stable society.

So we can learn from the highest ideals of the human family what God is like, but it is much safer, providing our view of him is not too distorted, to learn from God about the human family. And it is prime role of parents to teach their children about God so that they can grow up to be those who obey and honour him, and take their place as responsible and righteous members of the community and church. This teaching is done not just by words, but also by deeds and attitudes, and that is why we see the role as a priestly one, which it is vital for parents to understand and fulfil.

Let's try to summarise, then, the argument of these last two chapters. We've noted the spirit of the age which is one of rebellion against and lack of respect for authority. Nowhere is this more to be seen than in families, and we live in a time when family units are being more and more fragmented and when solid family values are laughed off as old fashioned. We've noted the tendency to see family as somehow 'bad', or at least irrelevant for the end of the twentieth century, but we've argued that in fact the ideal family is to be found in the church – the company of people who own God as their father. Thus the task which lies ahead of Christian families is to begin to stand against the erosion of family, and to reassert those relationships which God has modelled for us in his family.

We said that as far as children were concerned, the one thing which God seems to require of them is an attitude of obedience towards their parents, which will grow and mature into a proper attitude of obedience towards other authority figures in society. We agreed that love is important, but said that love which does not begin with obedience is no real love at all. Therefore the job of parents in trying to recreate family values is first and foremost to train their children to be obedient. In doing this they are revealing something important about the very nature of God and the way in which he expects us to relate to him.

Now for a really controversial comment: it is our conviction that the battle for obedience in our children is either lost or won by the time they reach the age of about two years old. By this stage they will have learnt a basic attitude to authority which says either that it is better all round to obey it, or that it is there to be kicked against and defeated. It is helpful for parents to understand that they have two very different tasks in hand: up to age two they are being *creative*; after that they may well have to turn instead to being *redemptive*. Fortunately God is in the business of both, and is very skilled at them, so our comments are in no way meant to be defeating and condemnatory. There is ample grace for redemption among those parents who feel they have failed, but it does help to understand that with older children the task in hand is a different one.

How might one go about this training in discipline? We're not going to tell you! This isn't a book about parenting, and any attempts on our part to try to write one would be pretty pale in comparison to some of the books already written. Dr James Dobson is the expert in this field, and we would recommend wholeheartedly his books on discipline.[1] But if pressed we might share with you a few principles which we have found useful so far, with the disclaimer that there is still plenty of time for it all to go wrong for us!

First of all we would say that it is a real battle. After our first son was born, our health visitor told us that we were in for a battle of wills, and that for our own sanity we needed to make up our minds right from the start that we were going to win. Time and again over the next couple of years we found this advice to be invaluable. So the first thing parents must do is to decide that they want and expect obedience, and not budge an inch until they get it. Secondly, we feel that loyalty to one another is vital, so that there is no chance for children to play us off one against the other. If we disagree, we'll talk about it later, but when the children are there we show at all times a united front!

Thirdly, we mean what we say, and we don't say anything we don't mean. If we promise a smack, we deliver. And we don't say things like, 'I'm going to lock you in the shed and go on holiday without you!' which we have no real intention of ever doing (tempting though it may seem at times). Thus children learn that our word is our bond. This applies to the word 'no' too. If we say they can't have sweets today, we mean it, and stamp down hard on any wingeing, 'Oh go on, why can't we?' We decided early never to let them know they could win us round if they kept on moaning long enough.

The other side of the coin to this is that if we promise them something good we try as hard as we can to make sure they actually get it. If we say we'll take them to the park, even though other subsequent events may make this difficult, we make sure we still take them, or at the very least renegotiate so that they can understand that it will now have to be tomorrow.

Above all, we try to discipline with love. When we have punished it has been a short sharp shock, and cuddles soon follow, so that it is clear that the relationship has not been broken, only temporarily damaged. We take seriously a theology of forgiveness, so that the response to 'I'm sorry' is never 'It doesn't matter'. We don't want them to grow up believing that sin doesn't matter, because it does. Rather the response is 'I forgive you', reflecting as it does the way in which God looks wrong full in the face and then forgives rather than pretending it's not important. And, as we've mentioned, we make sure that forgiveness is a two-way thing, and that we ask it of them when we've done something wrong.

Finally, we try to help them to understand the whole subject of discipline, so that it feels like a process in which we're all co-operating rather than something which we're doing to them. We've explained from an early age that we punish them because we love them, and we use the naughty, uncontrolled children we occasionally encounter on buses or wherever to help them understand that we're working together to prevent them ending up like that. They have actually told us that they understand what we're doing, and even said once that they'd prefer the occasional smack if it helped them to grow up into pleasant boys. The rebellious teenage years are still ahead of us (of which more later), so we can't yet claim that they are perfect or will be for life, but so far seems to be so good. At the very least we believe they have a basic orientation towards obedience rather then towards rebellion for its own sake, which is sadly more than can be said for many youngsters.

One final example may help to illustrate what we hope we've taught them. Recently they were playing with some friends on a rope swing in the woods. In the end it was time to move on, so John allowed them one last swing each. These they had, but Steve decided he wanted one more last swing. At the height of the arc he lost his grip, and fell about five feet onto the ground, landing on his head. A trip to casualty followed (with his brother singing the television theme tune as we went, in an attempt to keep him awake), followed by concussion and a suspected fractured skull. As it happened all was well, and after a couple of days recuperation he was as right as rain. We didn't go into a theology of divine punishment or anything, but Steve was quick to grasp the fact that had he obeyed me, the fall just would not have happened. This point was reinforced as he lay recovering on the settee watching '*Jaws – The Revenge*' the next day. The story involved a father telling his son not to go out in his boat because Jaws the killer-shark was about (having been miraculously reincarnated in the interests of box-office takings after his nasty end in Jaws I), the inevitable ignoring of the advice, and a climactic last-minute rescue before the son became lunch. Again, the boys were quick to grasp the significance, and at the moment any hint of disobedience from one brother is immediately greeted from the other with 'Don't do that or you'll get eaten by a shark!' They think it's funny, but they seem to have learnt the deadly serious message beneath it. If only Christians could learn the same about God!

## Notes

1. For example *Dare to Discipline* (Kingsway: Eastbourne, 1970), now revised as *The New Dare to Discipline*. Dr Dobson has written many useful books on the whole subject of parenting and family life, and videos of him lecturing are also available.

# CHAPTER FOUR

# A VISION FOR CHILDREN'S WORK

We said in the introduction that this book was about the whole work of the Holy Spirit with children. So far we've taken three chapters to talk about theology, parenting and the state of the family today, and you may be asking when we're going to get on with it and do 'tongues'. But we do feel it's important that parents, children's workers and church leaders are pulling together and working towards the same objectives: allowing the Holy Spirit to work in the lives of our children with his fruit and his gifts, and co-operating with him as he does so.

One of the objections raised against charismatic renewal in the church is that it is all froth with no depth or substance to it, and sadly this accusation has been true in some cases. Therefore it is important to reiterate what we said in the introduction: that this book is not about helping children to be charismatic; it's about helping them to be disciples. You can (and sadly many adults do) speak in tongues till the cows come home, but still have a heart turned away from God and a rebellious spirit. If, as we have argued, it is true that God requires obedience above all from children, then that must be because an obedient heart is the most fertile ground in which the fruit will grow. The gifts of the Spirit are important, but only in a context of the sort of sanctification which flows out of obedience.

If the church family is the context in which this vital work of the Spirit is to take place, it is important that the whole family has agreed standards and expectations, and that all can work together. We have found it helpful to set out clearly our vision for children's ministry, for several reasons.

First, we need constantly to remind ourselves what we're here for. This is true of us as a church, and we have both a vision statement and a 'strap-line', catchphrase or motto. The vision statement fits neatly (along with our church logo) onto a piece of A5 paper, and we put it wherever we can – onto our weekly notice-sheet, magazine or whatever. The strap-line, which is only six words long, goes in even more places, like the front cover of service books, headed notepaper, and so on. Thus we're always reminded of what we're trying to do.

Secondly, it's useful for checking out whether we are actually doing it or not. It helps us to stay pointing in the right direction if we have a clear target at which to aim. So we don't run the church by responding to the many new ideas which plop through the letter-box each year, or the multitude of plans or programmes which promise to revolutionise us, our worship, our pastoral care, or whatever. Rather we evaluate new ideas as to whether or not they will help us towards the fulfilment of our vision. It has also been very helpful in uncluttering the church to say that because some events or organisations aren't in line with the vision, then they have to go. Since the church council members were collectively responsible for the vision statement, they can all agree when some axing has to be done.

And thirdly, a clear vision can be clearly communicated. We are able to tell parents, particularly new ones, what we will be doing with their children if they leave them in our care, and why. We can say the same to the church leadership and so be helpfully accountable to them and, perhaps most important of all, we can tell prospective workers in our teams what we are about and what will be expected of them. We've put in a whole chapter about leaders, so we won't say any more now, but it is important to be able to let new members know what they're in for.

So here is our vision, carefully explained for you, although we would like to make the point strongly that it's not important that you work with our vision: it's vital instead that you work with yours, which may be very different. You can't import someone else's vision wholesale, but you can use it as a helpful basis in writing your own. Maybe ours will be helpful as you do this.

It's based around four 'r's: *Relationship, Resourcing, Relevance,* and *Really Good.* Each of these has two statements, which we'll set out and unpack. Here's how we present the whole thing:

---

# St James' Styvechale

## *Children's Ministry*

### 1) Relationship:

Children have a relationship with God.
They have an Enemy who is trying to spoil it.

### 2) Resourcing:

Children need to grow intellectually – knowing about God.
Children need to grow experientially – knowing God.

### 3) Relevance:

Children's ministry should invest for the future.
Children's ministry should have application now.

### 4) Really Good!

Children's ministry should be fun.
Children's ministry should have quality.

---

Now let's have a look at each of the headings:

**1) Relationship:** *children have a relationship with God*

In the first chapter we discussed the place of children with respect to the kingdom of God, and depending upon your point of view you may have agreed or not with the conclusions we reached and the point of view from which this book is written. We believe that whether or not they know it, children have a relationship with God: some will need telling about it, but others will need strengthening in it. Our job therefore is one of evangelism and nurture: to ensure that children enter into their inheritance as members of the kingdom, and to help them grow up in the things of the Spirit.

*They have an Enemy who is trying to spoil it*

Unfortunately there is another side to this relationship with God, and an Enemy who will do all he can to wreck it, terminally if possible. There is a battle on for the lives of our children and youngsters, and we want God to win. What's more, the battle is hotting up. You only have to watch the media, listen to music, visit schools or browse through toyshops to see that evil and occultism are coming more and more into the light of day. There is much more exposure to overt evil than we have known before, and the statistics suggest that the Enemy is gaining ground among children and youth. We were recently shocked by the torture and murder of two-year-old Jamie Bulger by two ten-year-olds. This is an extreme example, but the epidemic of juvenile crime and the steady loss of 400 youngsters each week from the church in this country shows that we have some work to do. The Enemy is slaughtering the spiritual life of children and teens in a way which is far more dramatic than any IRA bomb. What's more, he doesn't mind how early he gets them, while in the church we have thought and taught that the supernatural weapons which the Spirit gives us for warfare are only for those grown up enough to understand them. Our task, as we'll go on to explain, is to see that our children are fully resourced to fight back.

But what about the accusations of indoctrination which are so often thrown at the evangelical wing of the church? Isn't it akin to brainwashing to evangelise children, who are gullible and idealistic and easy prey for persuasion? And getting them into all this weird stuff about the Holy Spirit when they're too young to argue back is surely highly dangerous?

Brainwashing and indoctrination? Hold on a moment! Just look around at who and what else are seeking to influence our children's minds. Does the Enemy have any qualms about indoctrinating our children's minds with materialism, or rebellion, or violence, or the occult? No. He'll use whatever he can on children from as early as he can to bend them towards his way – the way that leads to destruction both now and for eternity. Why then should we hesitate to lead our children into the ways of righteousness and the things of God? This is nothing less than a satanically-inspired loss of nerve on the part of the church, and we need to unmask it as such as quickly as we can. If we don't believe that the gospel is the only thing which will benefit and bless our children, and if we don't believe that it is only a mass turning to Christ which will bring any hope at all to our broken world, then why on earth do we bother at all? Satan has no problem with brainwashing our children, and the church, duped by the liberal agenda of the culture, just lets him get on with it in the name of tolerance and freedom of thought. This is a class-one scandal, and this book is about how we fight it. If their relationship with God is to see the light of day and survive, children need all the help and equipment they can get.

## 2) Resourcing

We'll take the next two statements together: *children need to grow intellectually in knowing about God, and they need to grow experientially in knowing God.* It is important to understand that both these dimensions of growth need to be involved in the discipling of children (as they do with that of adults), because it is possible to know God in different ways. The French understand this: they have two words which mean 'to know'. *Savoir* means to know about, to have factual information, and part of the children's growth will mean that they learn more and more about the facts of the gospel, about Jesus and the kingdom. This is about their knowledge and use of the Bible, and this is where Sunday schools have traditionally been strong, and where in these days of increasing secularisation there is more need than ever before. Schools and homes are providing less and less in terms of what used to be called 'religious knowledge' (at least *Christian* religious knowledge: many children today know far more about the mosque and the gurdwara than they do about the church), and less and less children are in touch with churches to gain that information. Our children's ministry has an important informing role to a generation where ignorance is rife, and this role must never be decried.

But there is more to 'knowing' than just possessing facts. The French also talk in terms of *connaitre*, which is about a personal acquaintance with someone. Our children need not just an intellectual knowledge of Jesus, but also an experiential relationship with him.

This is where the partnership of word and Spirit is so important. We do want our children to know Bible stories, and to grow to be more like the God of whom they read. But we want them also to have experiences of God which touch their emotions and bodies as well as their minds. Our vision is to see children trained into a biblical knowledge of Jesus and the gospel, *and* an experiential grasping of their relationship with him. They will be taught from Scripture about the spiritual battle in which they're caught up, and they will be trained in the use of the supernatural weapons of warfare, both defensive and offensive.

Why is experiential as well as intellectual knowledge so important? Because it is one thing to cast doubt on someone's beliefs, but quite another to try to talk them out of their experiences. The story of the blind man in John chapter 9 illustrates this. It was easy for the authorities to tie him up in knots over his theology. Yes, it might have helped if he had had a better knowledge of who Jesus was, but the real clincher as far as he was concerned was his experience: 'One thing I do know. I was blind but now I see!' (John 9:25). Children who have seen miraculous healing on Sunday in church (and who may even have been the ones praying for or receiving it) will be harder to convince at school the next day that God doesn't exist.

The generation we are now seeing abandoning the church is the result of a previous generation which had some head knowledge but little experience of God. They began to ask (even if not to articulate) the question 'where is the reality behind all this?', and heard no answers. Like belief in Father Christmas, they simply grew out of it when they found no physical evidence that it was true. It does seem to be the case nowadays that the churches which are holding on to teenagers tend to be those which help them into a supernatural experience of the Spirit of God to go with their information about him. Information is great, but the hard facts prove that it hasn't been enough. So often young people are told that the armour and weapons which God has provided don't exist really, or at best they have them issued when the battle has already been raging for years. No wonder there are so few left alive to claim them.

### 3) Relevance

Here's our first statement under this heading: *children's ministry*

*should invest for the future.* We've already argued that society is
the worse for lack of obedience and the fruit of the Spirit among its
members, and that God has provided childhood as a time to learn,
and families as the place to teach, right values and character. We
have in our hands for a few precious years some young lives, and
they have the potential of being those who are special to God in his
redemptive work in the world as he brings in his kingdom. At the
moment, they're immature, unformed, noisy and fickle, but by
doing what we can to bring them closer to God, we hope to help
build into them Christian virtues which will be salt and light in our
dark and rotten world. We are very conscious of the privilege of
children's ministry, and hope and pray that some of those who have
been under our care will grow up to be great spiritual leaders in the
nation. We want to see them knowing God better and better in both
the ways we mentioned above, and growing more and more
effective in ministering for him.

This is not an uncommon aim, you may think, among children's
workers, but it needs to go side by side with the second statement:
*children's ministry should have application now.* Most Sunday
schools see their work as investing for the future, but few seem to
manage to make a more immediate impact. Chris' lasting
impression of her Sunday school years is that she was given lots of
information which she would one day find useful when she grew
up and became a *proper* Christian and church member. Her job was
to file it away in case she ever needed to find it. In reaction to this,
she is now concerned to make what she teaches relevant when the
children go home for Sunday lunch or are in school the next
morning.

Often the problem here is one of application. Bible stories are
left hanging in mid air, with no indication given of how they might
actually impact the children's lives. Jesus becomes a very grown-
up person, but not one who will be beside them in the night when
they have a bad dream, or in the class-room when their friends are
laughing at them. Little practical help is given to children to
encourage them to work out for themselves what it is they've
learnt.

Once we were teaching on the need to be articulate about Jesus,
as a prelude to some work on sharing their faith. Chris could have
just told a Bible story about a blind man or something, and ended

with the injunction to spread the word themselves, but she chose instead a more creative way of handling it. The children were asked to brain-storm as many names of Jesus as they could think of: King, Good Shepherd, the Vine, the Bread of Life, and so on. Then they were told to be still and quiet for a moment; Chris invited the Spirit to come on them, and they had to decide which *one* of these titles was their favourite. Then the whole group went on to construct a banner, which had 'Jesus' written in huge letters across the middle, and round the edge lots of little felt pictures which each child had done to illustrate their particular favourite: a crown, a crook, a bunch of grapes, a loaf or whatever.

When it was finished, the banner was taken and hung up in the church itself, where the adults met. The grown-ups were told about the making of the banner, and encouraged to find an opportunity to ask one of the children, 'Which is your little bit?' This led on to conversations about why they had chosen that particular image of Jesus, what it meant to them, and so on. Thus the children were not just told they should talk about Jesus: they were given practical help to begin to do it right now.

This had other advantages: not only did it avoid the temptation to store the information away until they were proper Christians later on and could act on it, it also removed the guilt with which most church members are weighed down as they listen to sermon after sermon and do absolutely nothing in response. Preachers and teachers may berate their congregations for their lack of action, and sometimes they may do so with justification, but often they could give a lot more help by making a response easier. Growth and learning become something which actually works, now, and a much more positive attitude to the whole process is engendered.

So our vision is to see children grow, in their closeness to God and in their effectiveness against the Enemy, in a way which has relevance for the present as well as for the future. We are aware of their limitations at the moment, but concerned to see them reach greater maturity.

### 4) Really good

Our last 'r' tells us not what our children's work must do, but what it must be like: *really good!*

Our first statement here is that *children's ministry should be fun*. Many of us adults have memories of enduring Sunday school rather than enjoying it. Many of us only kept going out of duty, or because our parents only kept taking us out of duty. Nowadays the concept of duty is virtually dead, and if we are to keep children coming back week by week for more, we will have to make them want to. There is so much competition, and we seldom hear children being enjoined to go out into all the world and spread the good news that there is a mini-rugby club in the park on Sunday mornings, and then to compel people to come in. In fact there's a hefty waiting list, because children really do want to join. Our aim has always been to create children's work which grows and gains a reputation far and wide. The only way to do this is to make it fun.

On one occasion the leader of a uniformed group, no doubt to impress us with his piety, was reassuring us that the children in his care didn't just mess around on all this secular stuff like knots and British Bulldog: 'We can be quiet and serious too.' This is exactly the image that 'church' has with those who seldom go: there is fun, and then there is religion, and never the twain shall meet. Our vision is to make religion fun.

So we teach through games. Recently, one of our team was doing some work with the younger children on 'families'. She asked them to think of as many things as they could which went on in families. They wrote a long list, which included nice things like cuddling, as well as others like fighting, divorce, jealousy and so on. Next they blew up loads of balloons, and wrote on each of them one word from the list. Then they all went outside, where the weather was conveniently blustery, and, as an act of prayer, simply let go of all the balloons which they didn't want in their families, and watched as they were blown away. No doubt there were a few surprised Sunday-morning gardeners around the parish wondering where this balloon had come from and why it should have 'People needing to phone Child-line' written on it, but for the children it was a tremendous piece of teaching. This kind of divergent thinking on the part of the leaders is a vital ingredient in turning 'religion' into 'fun'.

Other things too can add to the fun element. Mobility is one of them. Children are not required to sit still and listen all the time while an adult talks to them. Quite the opposite in fact: we often begin with a few minutes of aerobics to a praise tape. Colour is another: the leaders often choose their most colourful clothes for a Sunday morning, because it all creates the right atmosphere. And because we're an Anglican church, we often invite the congregation, including children, to dress up in the liturgical colour of the day. The vicar does, so why not them? So people wear red on Pentecost Sunday, purple for Advent, and so on. All in all, everything we do should point to the fact that you really can be serious and have fun at the same time.

The second 'really good' statement is this: *children's ministry should have quality*. The musicians, the OHP slides, the room in which we meet, the leaders, even the Little Things we make to take home at the end should be the best we can make them. Children enjoy making things, but they will not be proud of those they know were slung together from materials which the leaders had scraped together. Once we wanted to make a picture for the children to take home as a memory-aid for a Bible verse. Well in advance we asked one of the best artists in the church to come up with something, and he drew a line picture which we then photocopied (discarding the ones which were faint or had black blobs of toner on them). The children were then invited to bring in a favourite photo of themselves, and they coloured and decorated their sheets and stuck their photo in the middle. The finished article had their name, a large pair of outstretched hands holding their picture, and the words of Isaiah 49:16 (GNB): 'I have written your name on the palms of my hands.' This masterpiece remained on Steve's bedroom wall for months, as a daily reminder of God's faithfulness to him personally. Sadly the same is not true for many of the bits of junk taken home each week by the children of our churches. They can tell quality when they see it, and they'll value it much more than something made of a yoghurt pot and a loo-roll which their teacher has so obviously fished out of her swing-bin for them.

Quality is not just valued by children; it values them. It tells them that they are important to the church, that they aren't just to be given the fag-end of its human and material resources. Whether or not we like it, they are used to high quality in other areas. They watch videos, not film-strips. Their schools are full of brightly-coloured books with lots of pictures. They listen to their own tapes and CDs. We've got to compete if we're to keep them. Extra creativity, extra time, even a bit extra on the budget will repay our investment in terms of growth among our children.

So, *Relationship:* with God, but with the Enemy trying to interfere. *Resourcing:* helping children to grow in the closeness to God and their effectiveness in taking their stand against the devil, and giving them everything God has got to help them, now when they need it most. *Relevance:* for the future but for now too, and children's ministry which is *Really good* to go to and really good in quality. This is what we're trying to create in our children's ministry. Yours needn't be identical to this, it needn't even be as complicated, but it *must* be as clearly thought-out and as easily communicated.

That's what we're trying to do, but what do we actually teach? Having set out some principles, we'll now move on to get much more practical. We'll begin, as all good enterprises should, with prayer.

CHAPTER FIVE

# SPEAKING TO GOD

Our particular church tradition is, and has always been, one which values corporate vocal extempore prayer. That isn't to say that we see no value in other sorts: indeed we try to build in to our children a love for liturgy, a respect for silence, an appreciation of the use of the senses in prayer, and so on, but it does seem important to all Christians, and particularly to children, that they can cope with sharing with others in prayer by praying out loud and out of their hearts.

First of all there is Jesus' teaching in Matthew 18:19 about agreeing in prayer. This suggests, at the very least, that there is special power in intercessory prayer when two people can put their wills and hearts into it together. This does seem to presume that they can hear what it is they're agreeing about. Secondly, it builds in some kind of accountability. When people pray silently and individually there is no way whatsoever of knowing what it is they're praying for, to whom they think they're praying, or even indeed if they are praying at all (this is the problem we have with an unvaried diet of cathedral evensong-type worship). Praying is a corporate activity as well as an individual one, and we pray as members of a community, so we owe it to ourselves and the community that we get it right at least some of the time. In our Anglican services we have a point where we recite the creed together. This is a statement of our common beliefs, and no one would seriously suggest that we use instead three minutes' silence where we can all tell God individually what we think about him! We're accountable to one another and to the church community as a whole, and children especially have their faith formed to some degree by correction of misunderstandings which come to light as we hear them pray.

Thirdly, learning to pray aloud can help make God more real to us, and our relationship with him more immediate. There are times when we sit in silence with our family, or when we read passages of poetry or Shakespeare to each other (not all that many times, come to think of it, but some). But most of the time we just chat about what's going on, what we'd like, what we think about each other and so on. If we felt we could only converse with one another using someone else's words, or by silently contemplating each other, it could well have the effect of stinting communication between us a bit. Yet many Christians can only communicate with God via a book and language that is four-hundred years old. If children can be taught to talk to God naturally and easily, in the same sort of everyday language they might use with friends or family, it can't help but make them feel that God *is* a friend, and they *are* in his family.

And finally our observation would tell us that those who find it hard to talk aloud *to* God tend to be those who find it hard to talk *about* him. Teaching people to pray aloud will have spin-offs in that they'll learn to be more vocal about their faith and their Lord generally, and their witnessing will be helped. So we try to teach vocal prayer, along with other sorts, to the children in our care. It's not the only sort, and it's not the be-all-and-end-all, but a Christian who becomes paralysed at the prospect is not enjoying all the resources God has for them, and is living to some degree a handicapped spiritual life.

So how do you teach children to do it? And when? The answer to the second question is easy: as soon as they can talk. Childhood, and especially early childhood, is a phase of unparalleled growth and learning, and we can cash in on this tremendous capacity spiritually. If a child can talk, he or she can talk to God. So let's begin the lesson.

First, forget most of what you were taught as a child. 'Hands-together-eyes-closed' was a command designed to protect young children from distraction. But the effect it had on many of us was to tell us that prayer is something you do for a set time in a set way. If we did that and took Paul's command in 1 Thessalonians 5:17 to 'pray continually' seriously, we'd never be able to drive, prayer-walk or, incidentally, read from a prayer-book. It's a lot more helpful if we can use the 'distractions' as aids to prayer. This denial of the physical is particularly difficult for young children, who meet the world through eager senses.

Similarly, the terminology we use is important. To talk about 'praying' to very young children is to introduce a concept which is likely to be foreign to them, whereas they can relate much more easily to 'talking to God', since they already know what it is to 'talk to Mummy'; they're already half way there. In a nutshell, cut the super-spirituality and be natural with them.

Secondly, plan to build in both prayer-times and spontaneity. We referred in *Liturgy and Liberty* to a friend who used to say that it was easier to pray any time if you've first prayed sometime. Building in structured times for prayer will set children free for the spur-of-the-moment prayer which treats Jesus as a member of the family to whom we can talk at any moment without making a big fuss about it. We were driving off on holiday on one occasion, but our excitement was marred slightly by the presence of big black clouds glowering in the sky ahead of us. Suddenly, in the middle of a conversation about nothing in particular, one of the boys said, 'Dear Lord Jesus, please make the clouds go away so we can have a good holiday, Amen.' As parents and part-time theologians we knew of course that it wasn't as easy as that, but we were surprised about ten minutes later when the sun broke through and Steve said, 'There you are – isn't Jesus clever?' There's no doubt that times-when-we-are-going-to-talk-to-Jesus and spontaneous intercessions like that one go hand in hand, and we must build one in and be prepared for the other.

Thirdly, we have found it a helpful habit to insist that everyone prays every time we have a 'sometime'. This creates a climate and an expectation that everyone is involved, and more importantly, that we pray no matter how we feel – a vital lesson for adult Christians to have learnt. Obviously, this is most helpfully learnt within the family, but it can be done in Sunday groups too. Even if youngsters don't expect to pray out loud every day at home, you can still create the culture where they know they'll have to every week at church. This is only difficult, in our experience, at the beginning. Once the habit has been established and the culture created, children will fit into it quite happily.

That still hasn't answered the question about how you teach

children to pray out loud, but it has set out some helpful preconditions. What you do next is simply to construct what the educationalists call a 'small-steps programme' which will gradually take the children from where they are now to where you want them to be. In our last parish, one tier of children's ministry took them from three-and-a-half to five years old. First of all, the leaders set a goal: by the time the children moved up at five to the next group they should all be confident and unembarrassed in praying aloud with others. So there was an eighteen-month period to do the job. This time was broken down into five small steps which were worked through in small groups with a leader and three or four children. We found this to be a very leader-intensive process, but felt it important enough to invest in to such a high degree.

*Step 1.* The leaders did everything: chose a subject to pray about, prayed about it, and said 'Amen' at the end. The subject would be one which flowed wherever possible out of the teaching material of that particular day. After a while the children learnt to join in with the 'Amen'! The subjects for prayer were simple and familiar, and the leaders modelled short, jargon-free prayers.

*Step 2.* The leaders then asked the children to repeat the prayers phrase by phrase after them until they could do so without any problems. This and the 'Amen' from step one took them past an important landmark which many adult Christians have never passed; they broke the 'sound-barrier' and heard their own voices talking to God. And yet this major barrier, which seems totally unassailable to adults, was crossed with no problem at all by the three-year-olds.

*Step 3.* Now creativity began to come into play, and the children were asked to suggest items for prayer themselves. Then back to step two: the leaders would pray about the issues which they had raised, and they would repeat after them. This helped teach the children that they had to take responsibility for their own prayer.

*Step 4.* The next step was to get them to suggest issues for prayer, and then for the leaders to suggest how they might pray. This might be a set formula into which each of them could slot their own particular people or concerns: 'We're going to say in turn a prayer for one of our friends – "Dear Lord Jesus, please look after _____ this week, Amen." Now let's all say it with *our* friend's name in.' Or if they came up with an ill friend, for example, the leaders might tell them not so much what to pray as how to: 'You could ask Jesus to give Susie a good night's sleep so she feels better in the morning.' This is not then too inaccessible for them to put into their own words as a prayer. The leaders can now join heartily in the 'Amen'.

*Step 5.* Finally, they have all the equipment they need to think of an issue, compose a prayer about it and say it out loud. It may have taken them a year and a half to get there, but they've made it and the goal has been reached.

This is the model we used with very young children. Teaching them at an older age to begin praying out loud is similar in outline but it is possible to move more quickly through the stages. But we have discovered some additional practical tips. For example, prayers need to be kept short and to the point, and a formula like that above which can provide a framework for them is helpful at any age. When their turn comes the leaders will need to restrain their verbosity and shorten their prayers into the same formula in order to encourage rather than deskill the children. The ability of older children to write things down can be a help sometimes: they can write prayers and then read them aloud as a prelude to speaking them straight out of their heads.

We've also found ways to deal with two common fears which people have when learning to pray aloud: that they'll 'crash' with somebody else who begins their prayer at the same time, and that they won't be able to think of anything to say because someone else has prayed about the subject they had up their sleeve. First we use an object (often a Bible, although anything at all would do) which is passed round the circle rather like the conch in *Lord of the Flies*, signifying the inalienable right of whoever has it at the time to speak uninterrupted. Once it has gone round once and all have prayed, it can be put in the middle for anyone to pick up who wants to pray anything else. So far they haven't seemed worried about the possibility of two people 'crashing' as they grab for it at the same time.

The other thing is to teach about the importance of covering a subject in prayer from every angle. Thus if children (or adults, many of whom need to learn this lesson too) were praying for a girl who has gone from the church to work in Africa for a year, they could be encouraged not just to pray 'for Cathryn in Africa, Amen', but to pray in turn for her health, her friendships, the people she'll work with, settling in, getting used to the funny food, her Mum and Dad who'll miss her, and so on. This creative use of imagination in prayer can draw prayers out of children rather than restricting them because someone else has 'done' Cathryn.

Once they've learnt the basics, they can be led further along that journey into prayer which none of us has yet finished. They can be taught to expect answers, and be helped to identify them when they come. One resource for this is the 'prayer rainbow' which we currently use with our children's group, rather in the way that some adults use a prayer notebook. A large painted rainbow (which the children enjoyed making) fills the noticeboard, and onto it written prayers are pinned. The idea is that we can come back at a later stage to look for those things which have been answered, so that we can thank God, and those things which still need our attention, so that we can learn persistence in prayer. There is also the opportunity now and then to teach children about 'unanswered' prayer!

Then they can be taught about different ways of praying. The small-steps programme has provided them with the basic skills of prayer, which can then be enhanced by such things as liturgy, written prayers, the use of objects (stones and bits of play-dough were used on one occasion to bring to life some prayers around Ezekiel chapter 36:26), movement and dance as prayer, and so on. We used an enlarged map of the parish on one occasion so that children could stick pins into the appropriate place (like a kind of redeemed voodoo) and pray for their friends and neighbours to become Christians. We also invited children to bring in their school class photos so we could all pray for our friends, and we even prayed over a copy of the staff photo from each of the schools in our patch. They also made prayer cards to keep by their beds to encourage them to pray daily for one special person whom they were targeting. Different aspects of prayer can be taught with the use of a mnemonic such as ACTS (adoration, confession, thanksgiving, supplication), although of course the jargon needs to be unpacked. Maybe you could invent your own mnemonic together.

They can learn too about listening to God in prayer, and ministering in prayer to one another (each the subject of a later chapter). But we believe the basic skills of extempore prayer need to come first. Once a child has been taught to use a pencil and paper, he can then learn to draw, write, scribble, doodle, sketch, design and so on. But without the basics his artistic life will be severely hampered! So it is with the basics of communicating with God.

As well as helping children acquire the basic skills, we want to instil in them a love of praying which will stay with them all their lives. The secret is lots of variety and creativity, so that prayer in the group never gets to the point of being a drudge or a bore. Some of us adults who were brought up with, or even live now with, a much more restricted view of what prayer is and how we do it may need to broaden our own horizons in order to feed and excite the children in our care. Drawing, writing, moving, listening, silence, crying: all these activities and many besides can be prayer if done in a God-ward direction with the aim of communicating with our Father in heaven.[1]

Is all this a bit 'parental', imposing on children our way of doing things, and manipulating them so they learn to do it? Not if you believe ultimately that being able to pray is going to do them good. As parents we have no difficulty whatsoever with making our boys clean their teeth each day, and we will use fair means or foul to get it to happen, because we can see around us and have indeed felt at times within our own flesh the consequences of neglect! In the same way, when we look at the sick state of many Christians who have never learnt to converse naturally with their Lord, friend and brother, we don't mind how we help the children in our care to avoid such problems.

We can't leave this subject without a look at the subject of prayer in tongues. Colin Urquhart, one of the early pioneers of charismatic renewal in Britain in the sixties and seventies, wrote a chapter entitled 'Even Our Children' in his book about those early days, *When the Spirit Comes*, which tells of the experiences of the children of his church being 'baptised in the Spirit' and receiving the gift of tongues.[2] Twenty years ago this was the most controversial chapter of a controversial book, but it is fairly well accepted in charismatic circles nowadays that this gift is available for us and for our children. But we're not quite so experienced in knowing how to help children receive it. We won't enter here into any debate about the nature of tongues or the age-limits God is thought to have put on it; we'll simply report on our experience of leading children into it.[3]

The small-steps-programme for releasing children into tongues is pretty similar in principle to that used on adults, although of course children won't have half the hang-ups we do. It's helpful to think of five stages: *preparation, explanation, ministry, experimentation* and *follow-up*. An actual session might look something like this.

## 1) Preparation.

First of all there needs to be some sort of teaching which introduces the whole subject, and puts it on the personal agenda of the children. As with the subject of praying, we try to avoid any jargon. We talk about a 'special language' which God gives them to help them talk to him, and we demonstrate for them to hear: they seem to value this experience. But above all we try to help them understand that this is something which *they* can receive, and which they will find helpful in living for Jesus.

With adults, of course, this part is absolutely crucial. They will be filled with horrific fantasies, fed to them by the Enemy, about how tongues will get out of control, how they'll suddenly start doing it during evensong, or even worse on the bus to work. They'll also be under the more subtle but equally destructive illusion that it'll make them feel wonderfully ecstatic to pray in tongues, or that they'll never need to read their Bibles again now that they've got this hotline, or any of the myriad lies which those who use the gift know to be total nonsense, but about which we all worried before we began.

Children won't have many of these hang-ups at all, unless of course they've been fed them by ignorant adults, but there still needs to be some sort of information about the nature of the gift. This preparation should culminate in some opportunity for a personal response by each child.

## 2) Explanation

When it comes to praying for the children, they need at the outset to know what the actual ministry process will involve – this is what I'm going to do, this is what God will do, this is what you need to do, and this is what should happen.

They'll need to be told, for example, that they need to stand up but stay as relaxed as they can, and that those praying for them will ask God to send his Holy Spirit and give them the special language. They shouldn't try to do the praying themselves, but just think about Jesus. They may hear the people with them begin to speak in *their* language, and they may or may not feel funny, warm, wobbly or whatever. They'll need to be told that it's up to them to do the talking, and that they may need to practise a bit, just as they did when learning their native language, before it gets really fluent. Above all they need to be reassured that God is going to do something wonderful for them because he loves them so much. But keep it all as low key and matter of fact as you can. If you're in any way nervous or insecure, they'll pick it up and it'll get in the way.

### 3) Ministry

When all the explaining has been done you can proceed to praying for them. Again, the art here is to keep it as simple and as low key as you can. As before this is especially important in adults, who may be so tense that they can't even speak English, never mind the tongues of angels. Having seventeen people pressing your head down between your shoulders while shouting, 'Ooh, I'll have a shandy,' and commanding you to join in does not provide the best context to help a terrified British person to enter into the fullness of the Lord's blessing. When ministering to children this is totally unnecessary. A quick prayer, with a hand laid gently on their head, along the lines of: 'Dear Lord Jesus, please give Joey a special language to praise you, Amen,' is all that's required.

### 4) Experimentation

The fourth stage provides an opportunity for them to go off by themselves somewhere and try out what God has given them. They're usually told to get in a place where no one else can hear them, and try out loud to say or sing anything which comes into their head, no matter how faltering or how daft. We tend to give them a time limit for this, say five minutes, after which they must report back.

### 5) Follow-up

In this final phase, they come back and are asked if they feel God gave them the special language. As a rule, children will say, 'Yes, thank you,' and adults will say, 'Well, I did make a few noises but I was making it up myself.' Reassure them using Luke 11:13 that what they've got is the real thing, and warn them that before long the Enemy will whisper in their ear that it's just them making up gobbledegook, or even worse that it's a satanic counterfeit. Tell them it isn't, and that they should tell him to push off. We often make people promise faithfully that they'll get an egg-timer, and each day for the next week they'll set it for five minutes and make their funny noises, no matter how silly they feel, how strongly the Enemy tells them to stop, however boring it gets, or whatever. We guarantee that by the end of the week they'll be reasonably fluent, and we've not had many dissatisfied customers yet.

There are some people (only ever adults in our experience) who simply cannot get it to happen for them. Probably the least helpful thing to do is to pray again, only a bit harder. We usually encourage people to leave it, and not to let the whole thing become a big over-riding issue. They can have another go later, but they're still just as important and valuable to God, with or without tongues. But if we can get our children confident in the gift while they are still young and innocent of hang-ups, so much the better: we could be saving lots of frustration later on.

The children will, of course, need instruction about the use of the gift. There are plenty of good books on this subject which, although aimed at adults, can be useful resources for the leaders in taking the children forward.[4] They will also need opportunities to put into use the gift they have received, and appropriate space should be built into the programme and activities for this. We have found sessions of singing in the Spirit during worship times with the children to be helpful.

Leaders will need sensitivity in deciding how to deal with the parents of children who have received the gift: there is a tension between confidentiality and the need for sympathetic nurture of the children. Ideally, the children should be encouraged to tell their parents about the experience at the earliest opportunity, but leaders ought to have some kind of awareness of the range of likely responses, from that of those parents who will be overjoyed, via those who believe the gifts died out at the end of the apostolic age, to those who are not Christians at all and will think we've done something weird and sinister to their offspring. We'll have more to say on the delicate relationship with parents in chapter twelve.

The only final thing we would say here (because we've never seen it clearly taught anywhere else) is that we believe there are in fact not one but two gifts of tongues: *public* and *private* tongues. Once you understand this, it makes sense of the seemingly ambivalent material in 1 Corinthians chapters 12-14 where Paul can't seem to make up his mind whether he likes the gift or not, and it makes clear the different uses which the different gifts have. Paul wants us all to speak in *private* tongues (14:5), but not everyone does so *publicly* (12:30); rather only two or three should speak out *publicly* in a service (14:27). He thinks they would do well to lay off *public* tongues a bit and concentrate instead on the higher gifts like prophecy (14:5), yet he thanks God that he does it (presumably *privately*) more than any of them (14:18). The problem in Corinth was that *private* tongues was being used *publicly,* and a correct understanding of the difference can avoid excess on the one hand, but also encourage increase in the gift on the other. Children needn't be aware of all this controversy: they can just learn from the experience of the generation which pioneered renewal in the twentieth century and get it right from the start.

> Prayer is the simplest form of speech
> That infant lips can try;
> Prayer, the sublimest strains that reach
> The Majesty on high.

The words of James Montgomery's hymn emphasise the simplicity and yet the supreme importance of prayer in the life of the Christian disciple. Sadly, many of us live with crippled prayer-lives: the more we can do to save future generations from this fate by training them into good habits early, the better for them and for the kingdom of God.

## Notes

1. See Richard Foster's excellent book *Prayer* (Hodder and Stoughton: London, 1992) for an account of many different ways of praying.
2. Colin Urquhart, *When the Spirit Comes* (Hodder and Stoughton: London, 1974), p 59 ff.
3. Peter Lawrence, in *Doing What Comes Supernaturally* (Kingsway: Eastbourne, 1992), p 106 ff has a helpful methodology for minstering to people seeking the gift of tongues. Ours is slightly different but complementary.
4. We find among the most helpful:
   *Ibid passim*
   D. and R. Bennett, *The Holy Spirit and You* (Kingsway: Eastbourne, 1971), p 93 ff. (Twenty years old and very American, but still a classic.)
   D. Pytches, *Come Holy Spirit* (Hodder and Stoughton: London, 1985), p 62 ff. (A good guide from the Vineyard point of view.)
   D. Watson, *Discipleship* (Hodder and Stoughton: London, 1981), p 95 ff. (If we were only allowed the Bible plus one other book, this would be it!)

# CHAPTER SIX

# HEARING GOD

Once children are relaxed and competent at speaking to God, the next step is to move them into hearing him speak back. This leads us into the whole area of the prophetic, and before we talk about how to help children into it, we'd better define briefly what we mean by 'prophetic', since you will need to think through this complex area if you are to deal with it helpfully and accessibly.

The 'gift of prophecy' is one which Paul talks about at length in 1 Corinthians chapters 12 to 14. He seems quite keen on it, and tells his friends that they should seek it earnestly (1 Cor 14:1). But what is it? Well, it depends whom you ask.

In the early days of charismatic renewal in this country, it was easy to spot prophecy: someone stood up in church with their heart palpitating and their hair on end and said, 'My children, I love you,' or something. Prophecy as manifested in the local church was often (although not exclusively) fairly low key, but at times very powerful and edifying for all that. But there were other bits of the church which seemed to be in at a completely different level. When they sought to prophesy, it was for the nation, not just a home-group, and they seemed very interested in what was happening in Israel. They would spend time up mountains, and would return with revelations of world-shattering significance, even if few in the world ever got to hear about them.

And then, of course, there were the Kansas City Prophets, perhaps the most controversial prophetic movement of all in recent years. Their relationship with John Wimber gave them a ready platform in England, and you loved them or hated them (some of the other prophets hated them, or rather their approach to prophecy). A self-respecting prophet in the Kansas City tradition would prophesy about earthquakes, droughts and such like, and would seek individual prophecies which laid bare the secrets of a person's heart.[1]

Along with this came some discussion about when is a prophet not a prophet. The increased popularity of 'words of knowledge' has led some to ask about whether the dividing line between the different spiritual gifts in 1 Corinthians chapter 12 is as clear as we were taught in the sixties and seventies.

We mention all this because each of these different controversies has, in its own way, had the effect of deskilling the church every bit as much as it has of enabling, and maybe even more. No doubt there have been tremendous benefits from these different schools, and we ourselves have valued our exposure to most of them, but at the same time it can seem all a bit beyond mere mortals like us, and indeed like our children. If we are to lead children into prophetic gifts (and the whole thrust of this book is that we should) we must know what we understand ourselves to be leading them into, and we must have confidence that they can be led there. A requirement of earthquakes may not help us to be very confident!

Our approach of late has been to be very much more low key about the whole thing. For a start, we talk about 'the prophetic', 'prophetic gifts' or even, with John Wimber, 'revelatory gifts'. This takes us away from the idea of a specific 'gift of prophecy' which is not the same as a 'word of knowledge', a 'vision' or what have you. Instead we see a continuum by which God reveals information to us, which may be a long speech, a simple bit of knowledge, a picture, a series of moving pictures, or even just a vague impression or feeling. Was something a proper 'prophecy' or not? Who knows? It just told us something that God wanted to say. Seeing revelatory gifts in this way means that quite a few people, who would never call themselves 'prophets', do in fact move regularly in this area. This approach neither denies nor denigrates the ministry of those who clearly are 'prophets', moving in much greater revelatory power: it just allows us to begin where we are.

Next, our involvement with the phenomenon known as 'prophetic worship'[2] makes us question a view of prophecy as something which comes exclusively 'down' from God to us. Songs or music given spontaneously may contain what God wants to say to us, but may equally be expressions of what the Spirit living in our own hearts wants to say to God. Mary's prophetic outpouring known as the Magnificat (Lk 1:46-55) surely comes into this category. And even this may not be that hard and fast: one prophetic expression may contain both 'upwards' and 'downwards' elements.

So all in all we try to be pretty all inclusive about what the prophetic actually is. This means that it is much more accessible to children (and adults, incidentally) since it need not involve a long flow of spoken prose, adverse weather conditions, a particular minority interpretation of the Bible about the future of the Middle East, or the ability to read people's minds. It may do, of course, and there are clearly specially gifted 'prophets' whom God uses a great deal in these special kinds of ways, but most of us won't be like that. We can, however, still be 'prophetic', and we can help others to be too, especially our children. So how?

There are two things to take into account before we begin. The first is that to get prophecy firmly established in a church or a children's group takes time. Our boys enjoy jigsaw puzzles, and as far as they are concerned the more pieces the better. We often have one on the go, on a table on the landing where it won't have to be cleared up every meal time. This is referred to as their 'Big Term Project', and it can take months to complete, a few pieces at a time. Prophecy, and also, incidentally, nearly everything else we'll need to teach children, is a big term project. One of the most common mistakes among enthusiastic children's workers is to lose focus and try to make sure they get over everything they know about the subject in question in one session. Children simply don't learn that way (and neither, we suspect, do adults). So each session might be simply about putting a few pieces in place, so that they join onto the bits already there. The picture isn't finished, but it's beginning to take shape. Maybe an aim for a single jigsawing session might be just to finish that lady's face, or fill in the elephant's left ear, or whatever. So with the prophetic: learning is a process, and it'll take time. You can't spend a week on it and feel you've 'done' prophecy now.

The second thing to understand is that there is one significant difference between the prophetic and the other major spiritual gift we mentioned in the last chapter – tongues. An important thing to realise about tongues, and a thing which cuts both ways, is that it's pretty black and white. Apart from a brief learning stage (usually no longer than days) you can either do it or you can't. You've either done it before or you haven't, and you've generally noticed if you have. Therefore leading children into the manifestation of this gift is like making a new start. It's a breakthrough, a whole new experience, a quantum leap from where they were before. Prophetic gifts are different. The chances are that many children have already experienced something of it without knowing. This may have been anything from a vague sense of God in their minds to a full-blown word of knowledge. One four-year-old in a previous church went up to a lady in the congregation and announced confidently, 'There are *two* babies in your tummy!' The woman had in fact just discovered a few days previously that she was pregnant, and sure enough gave birth to twins some months later. The little girl had had no direct teaching on prophecy that we knew about, apart from being brought up by Spirit-filled parents, but it would have been a nonsense to begin teaching her as if she'd never had anything to do with the prophetic. Small children do quite often hear God, and so instructing them in prophecy is much more about naming and refining a phenomenon than introducing it.

So with that important background, how might we go about leading children on in this area? Here are eight useful headings under which we might proceed.

## 1. Teaching

Most of us who were brought up as Christians were often told that prayer was a two-way thing and that we should listen to God as well as speak to him. But few of us were ever given any idea about how this might happen, other than the possibility of Bible verses jumping out and hitting us. It is curious that with such a high degree of emphasis placed on the Bible, we failed to notice the sheer variety of ways in which God spoke to people then. Visions, dreams, angels, audible voices, even on one occasion a donkey: all these were used by God to speak to his people. So why the limit? Teaching on God speaking, and the ways in which we might hear him, needs to be built into the curriculum of the Children's Ministry, and it needs to be backed up with 'workshop' sessions where the children can begin to experience for themselves what they're learning about. We'll return to the importance of God's written word in the Bible later, but we shouldn't limit children to only one way of hearing him.

## 2. Preparing

Teaching provides a general background and puts the subject on the agenda, but before beginning to move into the prophetic, some more specific work needs to be done. As with tongues, children need to be told what might happen and what they have to do themselves. We teach them that revelation might come in one of five ways (ways we learnt from John Wimber's ministry): you see it (a mental picture), you read it (seeing written words in your mind's eye), you feel it (a sensation or pain in a particular part of your own body which may help identify a need for healing in someone else), you know it (just an overwhelming certainty about something), or you say it (it comes out of your mouth before your brain has had time to intervene and tell you you're making it up). Most of the children in our group would be able to tell you this, because it has been drummed into them over a period of time, and also because they would have experienced some of them for themselves.

Children need to understand as well that while God gives the prophecy, they are the prophets. Rarely is it like reading a ticker-tape which God has inspired verbatim: most of the time an idea or impression needs to be clothed in words or drawn out by a human being who will put the stamp of their own personality on it. Children may have heard adults who were brought up on the Authorised Version of the Bible prophesying in that kind of language, and that is fine for them, but it needs to be explained that there is no need to imitate the rather 'Old-Testament' style for a prophecy to be kosher. They can clothe it in words appropriate for their culture. It is probably true that this mixture of human and divine means that a pure one-hundred-degree proof prophecy is a very rare if not non-existent thing. Most of the time there will be a mixture of what is from God and what is from us (and not necessarily bad for that).

Children can be told to expect a sketchy revelation ('a snapshot' is more accessible terminology for them than 'a vision'), but that they can often get more by taking what they have got back to God and asking for further details. On one occasion our children's group was learning about words of knowledge, and were then going on to experiment. Chris prayed for God's Spirit to come and speak to them, and almost before she'd finished two children spoke up, one with a sense of someone with a hurt wrist, and the other with a picture of a house on fire. These were shared with the group, but no one seemed interested in responding. So they were invited to ask God for more details. The 'wrist' person said that the wrist in question had been hurt during PE at school last Friday, and the 'house' person knew that it wasn't an actual house on fire, but that someone was frightened about the possibility of their house catching fire. Immediately there was a response: someone had in fact hurt their wrist in PE on Friday, and they were prayed for for healing, and someone else had spent the night in his parents' bed after a particularly disturbing dream during which his house caught fire. He too was prayed for to break the grip of the lingering fear. Much of the time when our words don't seem to mean anything, it may be because we haven't taken this vital step of asking God for more.

As well as preparing children for what God may do, we also prepare them for what the Enemy will almost certainly do. We explain to them how much he doesn't want God's words spoken to us, since they are always to do us good and he only wants to do us harm, so he tells us every time God speaks that we are only making it up, and we'll feel silly if we tell people out loud. We train them to respond to the Enemy in the only way he deserves: by ignoring him and getting on with it anyway! They learn this lesson quickly when they see events like that described above taking place, and realise how much the Enemy would rob us of God's blessing if we let him.

## 3. Modelling

The third stage, which is not really a stage at all but should run concurrently with the first two, is that children should see the prophetic modelled. If yours is a switched-on sort of church where prophecy is a regular part of what goes on each Sunday, there won't be a problem here, but if your children are in fact way ahead of the adults, or if most of the serious adult spirituality takes place once the children are safely out of the way in their own groups, they may never have seen the prophetic working in a church service or group. This is where the leadership is important: they should be confident in moving in the prophetic so that the children can see it as well as learn about it.

## 4. Listening

After all the explaining has been done, children need an opportunity to practise it for themselves. Most commonly we would use worship as a context for hearing God, not just because we're more tuned in but because we take seriously a theology which says that God actually comes among us in a more manifest way when we worship him.[3] To those who would say that this is manipulative emotionalism, we would say first of all that it is scriptural (see 2 Kings 3:15), and secondly that the practice of hearing God in the context of worship enables us to practise and master the art of hearing him elsewhere.

So at the end of a worship time, we would ask God to come and speak to us. This may be very general or it may be more directed: sometimes the leaders will simply ask if anyone can see, read, feel or know anything, or wants to say anything, while on other occasions there may be a more specific target. Our children were doing a series on sharing their faith, and had talked about the need for constant targeted prayer. They had made and coloured little cards which said, 'Dear God, thank you that you love _____. Please help him/her to get to know you as a friend. Please help me to share you with him/her. Amen.' The idea was that this was kept by their beds as a daily reminder to pray. All that was required was for God to fill in the blank, so the children prayed and asked God to show them the one person he wanted this special prayer effort to go on. On other occasions healing may be on the agenda, so we may ask God to give specific words of knowledge like those mentioned above.

Other things can be used to encourage children to hear God. They can be put into small groups and asked, 'If God was here, what might he want to say to each of the other members of your foursome?' Not only does this encourage them to listen, but it also introduces them to the idea that God may give personal words for specific people. Another idea is to use physical objects. We mentioned in the previous chapter using stones and playdough to help us understand God's desire to give us new and soft hearts.

During a listening time after this exercise one little boy said that God had showed him how horrible he often was to his brother, and how it upset both his brother and God. There was prayer and ministry for forgiveness, and it subsequently proved to be a significant turning-point in the life of that family. On another occasion Chris had been playing with a large group of younger children with a parachute. She'd taught them previously how to hear God ('you see it, you read it, you feel it, you know it, you say it'), so they stopped parachuting and prayed for a moment for God to speak to them about himself through what they were doing. The range of things the children heard was amazing: from colour and joy to being wrapped up in God's love; being protected by him; one child even saw in the red panels a picture of Jesus' blood flowing down from the cross onto him to wash him clean. In the Bible everyday objects (the concordance doesn't mention parachutes, but pots get quite a good look in) are often the means of God's revelation, and they are a real gift to us when we work with young children.

## 5. Telling

Having given the opportunity for God to speak, it is important then to give the opportunity for the children to tell others what they've heard. One important factor to remember here is that children, especially young ones, will not usually think (or hear God) in words but in pictures. So it is helpful to have some pencils and paper handy for them to draw what it is they've seen in their minds. The older and more articulate among them may be able to use language to describe their revelations, but a picture-based sharing of what God has said is often more useful. It may also be helpful to tell a small sub-group before talking to the whole group, especially if it is a large one. To tell a few friends, with a trusted leader, feels much safer. The skilful leader can then tell the rest of the group in a way which draws the child out a bit: 'It was a *big* house you saw, wasn't it Sally?' Sally can then begin to fill in details in the presence of the whole group, which will build her confidence for next time.

## 6. Testing

The Bible is very clear that so-called prophetic revelations should be tested, and we would want to emphasise strongly that children should be taught the importance of this. We are only too well aware of the havoc that can be wrought in churches by 'prophets' who feel they are above correction or discernment (they often feel they're above the leadership of the church too). We have no desire to add to the revelation which God has given us once and for all in the Bible, and we teach them to value it and look to it as the final authority. But having said that, we would want to do all we can to be encouraging to children. To stand up publicly and denounce their first faltering attempts at sharing what they feel God has said to them as 'false prophecy' may put them off for life. Our aim, if we possibly can do so, is to endorse whatever it is they say and to congratulate them for it. There are times when correction is needed: when one little girl told us that God had said she needn't eat jam sandwiches if she didn't want to, we quickly discerned a domestic dispute over which she wanted divine backing! Even this was valuable since in the hands of an encouraging but creative leader it became the opportunity for a lesson about obeying your parents!

The basic understanding here is that it is more important to encourage the prophet than to get the prophecy word-perfect. A relaxed attitude will give children encouragement to try again, and the teaching they receive each week will be training them more and more to know God's heart and understand the kind of things he's likely to be saying. If they do get it wrong it's rarely malicious; it's just that they don't yet know him very well and therefore haven't learnt to filter out the bits which are much more from them than from him. They need help with this, not slapping down and 'correcting' in a way which will stop them ever trying again.


## 7. Responding

An important and quite liberating insight which came from John Wimber's teaching on the prophetic is the difference between revelation, interpretation and application. In a nutshell it means that the job of the 'prophet' is a bit like being a postman. When ours delivers the gas bill (which he seems to do with alarming regularity), he has got into the habit of simply sticking it through the letter box and going away again. We would be quite put out if he were to knock at the door, tell us how many therms we'd used and why, and insist that we stop what we're doing, go into town there and then, get some money out of the building society and pay the bill. His job is to deliver the message and let us decide what to do from there on. When (as does happen now and again) we bury it under a heap of other papers and forget about it, so that a nasty red letter from the gas board arrives, that is nothing to do with the postman; it's our problem.

If only some 'prophets' could learn this lesson! There is a common feeling that a hotline to God is the sole preserve of those with prophetic gifts, and an equally common set of disaster stories about what happens when the prophets try to take over the running of a church, writing off the leadership for the dullness of their spiritual ears (in other words, they won't do what we say God has told them to). The job of the 'prophet' is to hear God; they or others or the church as a whole need to discern the interpretation of that revelation, and the leadership need to decide how, if at all, the word is to be applied and what action needs to be taken. Children need to be taught early on that when they hear from God they offer it, and leave the rest to others. It may even be that they need to keep it and offer it to someone else at a later stage, although they won't be very good at this when they're young. Obviously with their 'encouraging' brief, the leaders will do all they can to find something about the word or picture to respond to, but children need to feel they've discharged their responsibility fully if they've just told someone. They don't even need to understand what they've said: only that someone else will, and that's up to God now.

Constant feedback is important so that the children can hear what has gone on during the week: our experience is that people seldom respond there and then to words of knowledge or prophecies, but will often come back later and say something like, 'I didn't like to say at the time, but that picture was just right for me.' This is infuriating, if understandable, but needn't rob us of the joy of having got something right if we make sure we do report back regularly. When we first began to move into words of knowledge we kept a careful note of words given and words responded to: we found over a period of about a year that we had something like a seventy-five per cent success rate, but that only about ten per cent of the words were claimed at the same time as they were given. Without this feedback we could have become very discouraged, and so can our children if they think that their so-called revelations are constantly meaningless.

They also need to learn, however, that they don't have a divine right to their prophecies being acted upon. That's up to the leaders. It may not be the case in the early stages that God will reveal his life-changing purposes for the church through the children (although of course he might), but to teach them these principles from the start will lay good foundations for the church of the future.

## 8. Refining

If prophecies need to be tested, prophets need to be refined. God may choose to give important messages through immature people, but they don't have to stay immature. This is true of all ages, but particularly so with children. The problem with them is that they're so young! Because of that, they tend to behave like children. One minute they may be rapt in worship, or giving a profound word from the Lord, but the next they'll be mucking about, pinching the little girl next to them and making rude noises with their bottoms. We recently heard one church leader telling about a service where some of the teenagers, lined up at the back of the church, had brought some blutak with them and spent the worship time modelling different shaped noses for themselves and each other. The leader caught the eye of one of them with a piercing glare, and he immediately joined in the worship and came forward a few minutes later to give a prophetic word which was formative in setting the whole direction of the children's ministry for the next couple of years.

Because there is a tendency for most adults to feel that spiritual gifts, and perhaps especially prophecy, are for saints of the higher degrees only, they can easily feel one of two things: that children who aspire to such things *are* saints of the higher degrees, or that since their behaviour shows clearly that they are not, the 'prophecies' can't be anything like genuine. In fact the truth is that they are just kids, and while God may *gift them* supernaturally from time to time, he seldom *grows them up* supernaturally, usually preferring to let nature and good parenting take its course. Thus in children we have a paradox: profound reverence and a model for spirituality which Jesus said adults should emulate, mixed up with mischief, immaturity and silliness, with the two succeeding each other by minutes or even seconds. The onus is again on the leaders to work at the big term project of discipleship, while neither despising the children's attempts to hear God, nor expecting them to be old before their time.

And when you come to think of it, is this very different from adults? How many people get up from kneeling at the communion rail in our churches, having received as the climax to their worship the bread and wine which speak of Christ's undying love, and the living sacrifices which we offer to him, only to be whispering to their neighbour a few moments later, 'Look at her hat! What does she look like? And have you heard about her daughter and the electric man? Well! . . .' Maybe the only difference is that children aren't so clever at being naughty quietly.

## Notes

1.  A good and sympathetic account of the Kansas City Prophets, their relationship with John Wimber, and the controversy which they stirred up, is given in David Pytches' *Some Said It Thundered* (Hodder and Stoughton: London, 1990). Others, less sympathetic, have renamed this book *Some Said They Blundered*.
2.  For details of this see J. King, *Leading Worship* (Kingsway: Eastbourne, 1988), p 114 ff, or D. Fellingham, *Worship Restored* (Kingsway: Eastbourne, 1987), p 40 ff.
3.  For an explanation of our theology of worship see J. Leach, *Liturgy and Liberty* (MARC: Eastbourne, 1989), p 21 ff.

CHAPTER SEVEN

# DOING THE WORKS OF GOD

Paul was toddling happily around the kitchen while Chris was at the sink, when there was a sudden cry of pain. She spun round to see Paul sitting on the floor with blood gushing from his hand and tears streaming down his face. Scooping him up, she tried to comfort him and to find out what had happened (we never did) and then ran the tap and put his hand under it. There was a large cut on one finger, and although she has no medical qualifications apart from a morbid addiction to *Casualty* on a Saturday evening, Chris knew that this was going to need stitching. So immediately she did what every mother would in such circumstances: pressed her finger to stop the flow of blood, shouted for Steve, and knelt down on the kitchen floor to pray. Steve (then aged about three or four) said something like, 'Dear Lord Jesus, please make Paul's finger better, Amen.' Chris let go, to find that the bleeding had stopped completely, and when she ran the tap again to clean it up, she was totally unable to find where the cut had been; there wasn't a mark.

(This is slightly off the subject, but you'll enjoy it, so have it for nothing. Our local house-church had a similar miracle where someone with a large gash on their hand was totally healed simply by holding it under the tap and praying. Like Paul, he didn't have a mark to show for it. When we Anglicans heard about this, we insisted that Coventry Christian Fellowship should open a shrine to the healing waters from the Holy Tap of Stoke. We suggested they run pilgrimages, sell little bottles containing water from The Tap, put a votive candle stand in the kitchen, and so on. Sadly they declined. No further miracles have been reported: could this be due to their disobedience to us? We may never know.)

When it comes to healing and the miraculous, children don't have

80

nearly as many hang-ups as adults do, so we need to be very careful as we explore this subject that we don't train children into our doubts. Steve has no problems with the healing ministry: he's done it himself many times. Their hang-ups lead Christians to have so many different views about and approaches to healing that the whole thing can be a bit like a minefield which we tiptoe through while our children skip around in uncaring abandon, never seeming to get blown up at all. Perhaps their lighter weight makes it easier for them, but those of us who are a bit more theologically obese can easily come to grief. So in this chapter we simply want to spell out some of the things we do, and why, without getting too deeply into arguments about the validity of healing. After that you'll find a continuation of the subject in the next chapter, which is a kind of rag-bag containing some of the less positive and attractive aspects of healing.

But first let's see if there is something we can all agree on. All the Christians we know would want to affirm broadly that *God is on the side of health*, but they would differ in their expectations about the *depth* or the *frequency* of healing. For some, a healing is not a proper one without abandoned crutches, disappearing tumours and redundant wheelchairs, or at the very least a headache which is no longer there. Others would say that healing is something we all need, all the time, until death finally heals us completely and we are made perfect in the presence of God. The first group might respond to this by calling it a get-out to explain why nobody ever actually gets better from an illness after prayer, and back and forth the discussion goes.

Similarly there is disagreement about the frequency and normality of healing. It *can* happen miraculously, of course, so the argument goes, but when it does it's the exception which proves the rule. It's a sovereign act of God, and it would be presumptuous to ask for one of those every Sunday. It might well be the exception, counter the others, but that's not how it should be, and we could see much more happening if only we could rid ourselves of unbelief and low expectations. Miraculous healing isn't the norm, sadly, but it should be. Again the arguments go on.

Perhaps there is a point of agreement, though. Whatever we believe, can we doubt that God would like to do more than we see at present? Whether a lot more or only a bit more, and whether greater depth or greater physical effectiveness, are secondary questions. But all of us would surely like to see more people healed more completely through prayer. If we can agree on that, we can begin to move forward and ask how we can see it and how we can let little children lead us.

First of all, we work with a particular model because it is one we have found to be accessible. We found it accessible to adults originally, and it was only as we began to move into this area with children that we realised just how helpful it was to them. But in choosing one model, we have also had to discard others, not because we think there is no place for them but because they don't feel right for our context.

So we don't go, for example, for what many would call the 'sacramental' model. Tending to come from a more high-church background, this model is often based around the Eucharist or Holy Communion service, and is very quiet, peaceful and orderly. The laying-on-of-hands is administered by the priest and other ministers while the recipients kneel at the altar-rail, and the expectation is that God's healing power would touch the seekers in terms of greater peace, greater strength to cope with the illness, and other inner qualities. While there might be a dramatic and miraculous healing at such services, it is not expected to be the norm. There is often a semantic distinction drawn between 'curing', which is the removal of an illness, and 'healing', which is a much deeper touch of the power of God on the soul, even though the physical symptoms may remain unchanged. The laying-on-of-hands often goes alongside counselling.

We don't tend to go along with this approach because it is not at all child-friendly. The quiet peace of a typical 'healing service' would not be helpful to youngsters (and neither would their presence be to others), and the apparent lack of anything tangible happening would be hard for them. Children need to see something to believe it, and the benefits of getting 'courage and hope in their troubles' . . . and 'the joy of your salvation'[1] would, frankly, leave them unmoved, especially if their tummy ache was still there. And of course the more theologically astute would remind us that in the stories in the Gospels Jesus didn't give peace to people who were ill; he made them better! There could be a credibility problem here for those children who are still naive enough to believe the Bible.

Neither do we find it helpful to give the impression that healing is something administered by a big, famous, charismatic and often very noisy 'healer' who lives in a tent and in front of whom we all have to queue so that we can fall over on the floor. While spectacular to watch, and even at times spectacular in its results, this model tells children that this is something others do to them. We want to give a different message.

So the model we have found to be most helpful is that taught by John Wimber and the Vineyard movement. It is charismatic without needing to be noisy and violent; it has biblical-sized high expectations but also a satisfying theology of failure, and any three-year-old can do it. One of John Wimber's greatest gifts is the ability to analyse and teach that which we have already referred to as 'small steps programmes', and his five-stage pattern for the healing ministry is one which we have easily adapted for use among children.[2] So what might we actually do?

## 1. Identification

For whom do we pray? Sometimes, as we've already mentioned, the need for prayer may be identified through a bit of information which comes out of a time of listening to God. At other times a problem may come to light through discussion, or a request for prayer. Sometimes the leaders can simply ask if anyone has something about which they'd like prayer. Any of these may come from a look at a healing miracle in the Bible: the stories are great faith-builders. If ministry is built into the normal programme, and particularly if children are used to seeing adults ministering to one another in big church, it soon becomes a part of the culture, and holds no embarrassment. Children are also gloriously free from the pride which causes adults to struggle on without admitting or opening up their need for prayer, and will be only too glad to be on the receiving end of ministry.

As with adults the nature of the need may vary, and it is to the credit of the sacramental model that it challenges our preoccupation with the merely physical and outward. Leaders need to develop among their children an understanding that any kind of problem is fair game for the power of the Spirit, and we're just as happy to pray for verrucas as for their argument with Tracey at school or their violin exam the next day. This doesn't cheapen a serious and reverent ministry, as some would suggest; it models a God who cares about every area of their life and can make a difference in any of them.

## 2. Explanation

Having found your victim, there is once again the need for some kind of explanation of what is about to happen. As usual, picture language is most helpful for children. 'You've asked Jesus for something,' we might say, 'and now we're going to ask him as well. So you need to be very quiet for a while, close your eyes, stand still and hold out your hands so that Jesus can give you what we're asking for. You don't need to do any more praying: we'll do that bit; you just concentrate on thinking about Jesus and what he's going to put into your hands.' (We often encourage adults, too, over this last point by reminding them that if they were having an operation they wouldn't be helping, so they can safely leave the praying to us.)

The other children also need some explanation about their part. We tell them to stand in a group around Ben, for whom we're praying, and put their hands gently on him without pressing or hurting him. We also tell them to pray with their eyes open because they will be able to see what God is doing to Ben.

## 3. Invitation

We then encourage one of them to pray one short prayer: 'Come Holy Spirit,' This invitation or calling down of the Spirit is a hallmark of Vineyard-style ministry, which we argue for at some length in *Liturgy and Liberty*.[3] It's not that God isn't there all the time, but that at some times his presence is more manifest: he's not just around, but he's actually doing something and we know it, and can feel and see it. It's this kind of powerful presence that we seek as we begin to minister to one another. We teach the children how to see the presence of God, and we teach them to wait quietly until they can see it. So, for example, they may see physical changes come over their victim, such as breathing deepening, eyelids fluttering, swaying, shaking or trembling, a facial relaxation or glow, or even 'resting in the Spirit' as they fall to the floor under God's power.

It is important to get over our natural adult reaction to these manifestations as 'weird' and teach children to expect to see them as marks of the Spirit's presence, and to welcome them. If there is any sense of fear initially (and if there is the chances are they'll have caught it from the adults) a quick interview afterwards with the victim will reassure them that it all felt lovely. As children grow in this ministry they can be taught a bit more about what different sorts of physical manifestations might mean, but they do need to know that it will achieve very little to begin praying before there is clear evidence that God has shown up.

## 4. Prayer

With adults this bit can go on for hours, but with children it is short and sweet. Those ministering can be encouraged simply to ask God to do what it is they're after, or to address the condition and tell it to go, or the bit of the body telling it to be healed in the name of Jesus. The leader may ask who'd like to pray, or may ask one of the children, 'Would you like to?' (meaning: 'Will you, please?'). The other children can be encouraged to pray quietly, in their special prayer-language if Jesus has given them one. The leaders need to find the right balance between modelling the ministry, encouraging the children into it, and stepping back and letting them get on with it. There is always the temptation to do everything for them, but that will prevent growth rather than facilitating it.

As with the more ordinary prayer we discussed in chapter five, it can be helpful to teach children set phrases to use when praying. So to 'break the power of' fear or oppression; to 'command' bits of the body to be healed, or to move back into place; to 'set free' the victim from their illness, to 'cut them off' from unhelpful family ties: all these phrases can be taught in their appropriate context, while of course never neglecting to teach that it is the power of God which heals and not our words. Children must be taught that healing is first and foremost about listening to God, which hopefully they learnt to do in the last chapter! But having particular phrases in their vocabulary helps them to select something appropriate when God has spoken to them.

As specific prayer begins, there may be more physical manifestations or there may not, but there is almost always some sense of power having been moved around (difficult to explain, but very real to experience). Children are quite good at this bit because they don't seem to suffer from the temptation to talk God into doing what they want him to do by listing all the reasons why this is a particularly meritorious case and deserving of his attention. They seem to be perfectly happy with 'Dear Jesus, please make Ben's sore throat better, Amen', or 'We tell this poor arm to get better', which is a coincidence because that's just how Jesus seemed to pray when he was ministering healing.

## 5. Feedback

Another characteristic of John Wimber's approach is the desire to know how you've done. It isn't enough just to pray and then move on; we need to talk to the victim, ask if they felt anything, if the pain is better, if Jesus showed them anything or spoke to them, or whatever. Children are almost always encouraging, in our experience, and will have felt God touch them in a very welcome and positive way, even if full and complete healing has yet to be seen. Jesus is frequently very powerfully present, and his presence is discerned in tangible ways. Adults will commonly tell you that as a result of your ministry they feel much more peaceful: children are far more likely to have seen Jesus holding them or walking into the difficult situation ahead of them. It may be that stages four and five can go round a few times with more prayer and more talking about what has or hasn't happened, although our experience is that this is less helpful (and indeed less necessary) with children.

And finally don't forget the longer-term feedback. Testimony is important in building faith and encouraging more prayer and ministry for others, as well as for proving to children that God is alive and well and living in them. You don't have to be a vicar or a German with a funny name: *you* can heal too!

So that's the process, and it takes at the most ten minutes. It's easy to learn and accessible to try out, and we hope you'll find it something you can begin to do yourself if you don't already. But that is the easy bit, and we do need to go on and say a bit more about helping children to move on in healing, both practically and theologically. Three areas particularly demand our attention: growing, failing and a quick word about deliverance and the demonic.

## Growing

Quite a few books have been written which very helpfully lead adults further on in the healing ministry (in the Vineyard model in particular) and some of them are detailed in the endnotes. It ought to be possible to write a children's version of them, but a more helpful way would be for leaders to immerse themselves in the theory and practice of the healing ministry, and then use their understanding of children to translate it all to their level and to teach it at their level. This is, after all, how teachers are trained: Chris spent four years at college, and her estimate is that seventy per cent of the time was spent on history and only thirty per cent on learning about children and education. That's why children's work must never be seen as the soft option in the church: leaders need to be every bit as familiar with the Bible, theology and the things of the Spirit as anyone else, and then familiar with how children think and learn as well. Being 'good with children' is nowhere near enough. (More of this in chapter ten.)

So what's the curriculum? Greater power in physical healing, including greater sensitivity about the real nature of the problem, which, as any GP or therapist will tell you, can be very different from that which is presented; an understanding of inner healing and dealing with hurts, sins or traumas from the past which are having a detrimental effect on life in the present; skill in listening to God so that prayer is pin-pointed and focussed, rather than vague and general; patience and persistence; dealing lovingly and respectfully with your victim; spiritual warfare; the power of forgiveness and absolution; when to use things like oil or holy water; All these and more will be areas for the leaders to explore and learn about, so that they become at least to some degree experts in them.

Then what about children? We've already mentioned that they have fewer theological hang-ups, and that if a Bible story tells them that Jesus healed someone, then he did, and if he did, he still can. So we won't put our fears, hesitations and theological questions onto them, but we'll try to do what Jesus told us and become more like them in their simplicity of faith. We also know that children think much more pictorially than theoretically, so we will explain and teach in more concrete terms, and use images and illustrations which will relate to their world. We will know if we've worked with them for more than five minutes that they have a shorter concentration span than we do, so we won't expect them to feel happy with long periods of silent prayer, and we won't get surprised or offended if they lose interest and wander off after a while. Any children's leader worth their salt will build this understanding into all they try to teach, and the healing ministry needs to be treated in exactly the same way.

That's the nice bit, then. But what when it isn't quite so perfect? We'll continue in the next chapter to look at helping children cope with failure and death.

### Notes

1. From the Intercessions section of the Anglican Rite A Communion Service in the *Alternative Service Book 1980*, p 125.
2. For definitive accounts of John Wimber's healing methodology, see his *Power Healing* (Hodder and Stoughton: London, 1986) and David Pytches' *Come Holy Spirit* (Hodder and Stoughton: London, 1985). Also very helpful is Peter Lawrence, *Doing What Comes Supernaturally* (Kingsway: Eastbourne, 1992).
3. John Leach, *Liturgy and Liberty* (MARC: Eastbourne, 1989), p 26 ff.

# CHAPTER EIGHT

# FAILURE, DEATH AND DEMONS

We wouldn't want you to have got the wrong impression from reading the last chapter. In fact you might have got either one of two wrong impressions: that we are tremendously successful at the healing ministry (we're not) or that since we're not tremendously successful at it but still want to teach it to children, we're living in a kind of triumphalistic cloud-cuckoo land (we're not, but we do believe in Christ's triumph, and we'd rather live with that than the pessimistic death-wish of some sections of the church). In fact, as we come to address the question of failure, we can say with some pride that this is a subject we know a lot about, having had quite a large amount of experience in it.

This area is a huge issue for adults. Some schools of thought would want to put 'failure' in inverted commas, since nothing is really failure as far as God is concerned. Others (like us) would want to say that if we've asked for someone to get out of their wheelchair and walk and they haven't, it's the closest thing to failure we've ever experienced. If that isn't failure, we're not quite sure what is! So all sorts of questions spring up to get us, like whose failure it was, why do we fail, does God ever fail and, at a deeper level, what does it say about me that I find the concept of having failed so distressing that I need to put it in inverted commas to pretend it hasn't really happened?

Children seem to have no such traumas. Perhaps it is because they fail all the time and so are quite used to it. 'Mummy, can I have some sweets?' goes the conversation when Mummy pops in for her *Radio Times*. 'No, not today,' comes the reply. This is total and abject failure. They wanted sweets and have failed entirely, one hundred per cent, to get any. Not a single sweet. Zilch. Let's face

it; that's what most of us would call failure. But children do seem
to be very good at being philosophical about it. Rarely do they go
into a deep depression and doubt whether, in fact, Mummy really
exists at all. Seldom does this kind of event lead them to question
the love of their Mum, or her power to give them some sweets if it
be her will. They seem to be very good at forgetting the whole
incident completely in a few minutes (unless of course their parents
have trained them into whining and grizzling until they get what
they want), and neither does it put them off asking the self-same
question next time they're in the newsagent's. Were they able to
articulate it, they'd probably tell you that Mummy did love them,
but chose not to give them what they wanted there and then for any
number of unspecified reasons which they might or might not
understand. Better luck next time.

Now we're not wanting to illustrate a God who is whimsical and
who sometimes withholds from us things we'd like for reasons we
don't understand. It's much more complex than that. We simply
want to make the point that not getting what they want is part and
parcel of a child's life, and quite honestly it's no big deal. So much
of our agonised adult theologising about failure in the healing
ministry is irrelevant to them. But there are things we can helpfully
say, not in order to explain their mistakes but to encourage
persistence.

We try to teach children about the kingdom of God and the battle
that is going on as it breaks into our world. We might talk about the
Enemy, the Prince of this world who keeps people locked up in a
prison, hurts them and frightens them, but also about Jesus, the
rightful King, who has come back to fight him, to release those he's
locked up, and get them into his army so that they can help release
even more people. To avoid dualism we'd make it clear that the
castle has been stormed and the Enemy bound up, but that the
fighting still goes on until that day when Jesus' victory will be
complete. So every time we pray for healing we're fighting a battle,
and there's an Enemy who doesn't want Billy's arm to get better
because he rather enjoys people hurting and anyway he doesn't
want that Jesus getting any more glory.

Then we might talk about why soldiers on earth might lose a
battle from time to time: they're too tired or worn out; they don't
know how to use their weapons properly; they're too busy fighting

among themselves to fight the enemy; they're not listening to their orders well enough, and so on. So what might they do? Keep trying and get better at it. This seems to us a perfectly good and biblical theology of failure, with the added advantage that it is very pictorial and accessible to youngsters. And above all they can be taught that however much they fail, God still loves them, is for them and wants them to get back into the battle. So when healing does come they can be taught to rejoice and thank God for it, and when it doesn't they can be taught to take it in their stride and keep going. If we feel devastated, we musn't let it show too much.

Along with failure comes the whole area of death. In a previous parish we struggled in prayer over a little boy of two who had a brain tumour. The battle seemed to ebb and flow for months, with remission and relapse, successful therapy and impossible surgery. Then finally Richard's condition deteriorated and a few days later he died, on our Steve's fourth birthday. He had been a regular member of the children's group, so it was natural that loads of his little friends should be at the funeral, joining in with his favourite songs, like 'God's not dead, No! He is alive'.

Another church we know had a similar battle over a boy of fourteen, also with a brain tumour. For six months the church prayed, and a regular prayer-meeting for the children took place (at their request), but finally he too died – on Good Friday at 3 p.m. as it happened – and the shock waves rocked the whole life of the church for some time. So what about children? Is it a danger to their faith to get their expectations up and then find that God doesn't deliver the goods? After all, the one advantage of a liberal interpretation of the Bible with no miracles is that there are no disappointments either. How do we deal in a charismatic way with children and death?

First of all we'd want to teach our children that death is real, that it's a fact of life, and that we'll all face it, in others first and then finally for ourselves. Neither would we want to stifle the grieving process which is every bit as important for children as it is for adults, if somewhat shorter. So death, and especially the death of someone for whom they've prayed, is a real tragedy as far as we are concerned.

But it is our experience that if they are allowed to talk openly about it, children quickly become very philosophical about loss.

They can usually talk in quite a matter-of-fact way about their little sister who died: it doesn't seem to be a very big deal. Our experience in schools' work is that children are glad to tell the class any stories they have about loss. So our task as children's-work leaders is to overcome our natural adult reluctance and encourage the subject to be aired. There will be times when the subject is difficult for us personally, but if the children do see us shedding a tear or two it won't harm them; we can tell our story and it'll bring us all closer and teach them some valuable lessons which may help prevent them clamming up emotionally when they grow up.

Spiritually, we find that most children have a certainty about the fact that their dead friend or relative are now with Jesus, especially in the case of a dead baby or child. It seems almost as if there is an instinctive faith in them, which of course we've argued that there is. Even the children of non-Christian parents have such a certainty. They may have been told so by their parents in order to comfort them, and the parents may or may not actually believe it for themselves, however much they'd like to, but this is one occasion where folk-religion is a positive thing, and can reinforce the children's natural faith. If they've prayed and seen death nevertheless, they seem to take that in their stride too. We'd like to be able to tell you exactly how to cope with their devastation and answer all the agonising theological questions, but I'm afraid we can't; we've never had to. It seems to be only adults who get into a mess with things like that. 'God chose not to heal him because he had a better plan,' said one fourteen-year-old. 'He chose him to go and be with him instead.' 'Disappointment but not devastation' was how the reaction of the children was described after their failure to see the fourteen-year-old healed. 'God knows better than we do, so we don't have to question. He's gone to be with Jesus, so we don't have anything to be sad about any more.' The fact that he had died at exactly the day and time that Jesus had was of great significance to the children. There was not the slightest trace of them losing faith, being angry with God or asking agonised questions. Instead there was a joy that God's will had been worked out, and paradoxically a new determination to learn to pray better in the future. Only adults, it seems, have big problems with death.

But there is one more area around this subject where adults have a tremendous amount to learn from children. As we wrote this bit we discussed with our boys their views on death, and the thing which shone through all their answers was the certainty that life with Jesus is a lot better than life on earth now. Although this may reflect their feelings about life in a vicarage, it also suggests that they really do take seriously what the Bible says about heaven, and it really challenges most of the earth-bound Christianity which we see lived out in our churches. 'For me,' said St Paul, 'to live is Christ and to die is gain. I desire to depart and be with Christ, which is better by far' (Phil 1:21,23). Children really do seem to believe that this is true; as we get older, it appears, we become more and more tangled up in this life, more and more reluctant to leave it, and more and more upset about those who have. Children have so much to teach us about freedom in this area, and they really do believe that their little friends who have died are having a much better time than they are. After all, they will tell you longingly, there aren't any brussels sprouts in heaven.

One final area concerns the demonic. We believe in the reality of the devil and his minions, because the Bible and our own experience have convinced us of it. Unlike some Christians, we're not that interested in gaining more and more esoteric information about the Enemy, and we certainly don't want to teach children things which go beyond what the Bible teaches,[1] but neither can we ignore this whole subject. The Bible doesn't do that either. So does it impinge on our ministry to children? And is it something so awful that we need to keep them right away from it?

A bit of theology and Greek to begin with might be in order. There is a term which needs to be banned from our vocabulary: 'demon-possession'. It is not a term which has any Greek or Hebrew antecedents, and its common use, even in translations of the Bible which ought to know better, has told us two very big lies about spiritual warfare. The first is that the only thing demons do to people is make them roll around on the floor screaming and foaming at the mouth, and the second is that since this kind of behaviour is pretty rare in most churches, so are demons. Neither of these has any basis in fact. So we have a rather different theology, based on the fact that the Greek word *daimonizomai*, used in the New Testament, can best be translated 'demonised' or 'demon-influenced'. How do Satan and demons influence us? In all sorts of ways, very few of which result in teeth-marks on the church pews.

When we're tempted, for example, and have given in, we have been influenced by demons. This is incredibly liberating, because all at once we realise that we're all demonised. This isn't some loony rolling round a graveyard; it's me, and I'm still here to tell the tale! Demons can oppress us with doubts and fears, can cause physical illness, can lie to us and make us believe it, and yes, in some extreme cases can cause us to react violently and obscenely against the presence of Jesus. But there's a spectrum. In all the Gospels there is only one occasion when Jesus met what we would think of as a classically 'demon-possessed' man, with dramatic results (especially for the pig-farmer – imagine him filling in his insurance claim). Only one incident out of three years' ministry. Yet there were many times when he dealt with the demonic in much more down-to-earth ways, in fact, as the writers tell us, 'with a word'.

What this means is that the whole area of deliverance is no big deal. If you were a GP, you'd spend the vast majority of your time on conditions which could be dealt with simply by a few pills, a day or two off work, or a quick jab. Occasionally you'd come across something much more serious, and your job would be to recognise it, but not necessarily to treat it. There are specially trained consultants for that. In the same way most of the demonisation you'll come across will be routine stuff which a quick prayer or command will deal with perfectly well, and there is no reason whatsoever why children can't be involved in this ministry. You'll have to recognise more serious situations, and have some basic knowledge of how to deal with them, but they won't crop up that often, or at least if they do you'll begin to ask whether God might be giving you a special ministry!

It is clear from the New Testament that Jesus ministered deliverance to children, and it is likely that children were around while he was doing so. On one occasion (Mt 15:21-28) he did so from a distance, and on another (Mk 9:14-29) there was direct ministry, again at the request of a parent, and quite a dramatic manifestation of the demonic before the boy was finally set free.

We have occasionally prayed for children directly for deliverance, but most often we've experienced the power of God to set them free without their ever having known anything about the ministry. Praying for them from a distance, and particularly the agreement of a couple of people in prayer, can be very effective. Some time after our boys were born, Chris found a job in a local school where she did part-time 'special needs' work. She had previously done a few odd days' supply teaching there, but didn't really know the characters or backgrounds involved. On her first day she was working with a little boy of nine who had reading and behaviour difficulties, when God said to her quite clearly that he had a severe problem with rejection (the boy, not God, although he probably does too if the truth be known). Without James noticing and without touching him (which of course teachers wouldn't be allowed to do these days), she prayed a silent prayer of deliverance to break the power of rejection over him. From that day on he began to improve. As Chris found out more about the family background she realised just how right her supernatural information had been, and at his case-conference at the end of the year no one could understand why there had been such a dramatic improvement; it went far beyond anything which could have been projected for him.

Another incident involved Chris praying from a distance with another teacher who was also a member of the healing team at the church we were in at the time. In her class there was a girl who showed severe and bizarre temper tantrums. She was always rude and unco-operative, but if told off even slightly she would fly into a rage, and on one occasion she began throwing chairs around the classroom, endangering other children. Even if she was not disciplined, she would have a tantrum every day at three-twenty just before school ended, when the teacher spent a few moments with the class praying (you can just about get away with that in a church school). The behaviour would get worse whenever they prayed, or in RE lesson, or on trips to the church. Her teacher felt torn: she didn't want to let her rule and get away without discipline, but at the same time she could see another child being injured if she provoked a violent episode. The rules about physical contact with children hampered her severely too. Finally, knowing Chris' involvement in this area, she sought her advice. Could there be something demonic in Jennifer's background which made her act in such antisocial ways? The two of them decided to pray together about it.

They handled the session exactly as they would have done had they been faced with a person asking for deliverance, but without

Jennifer actually being present. They invited the Spirit to come on her, wherever she was, and asked God for words of knowledge about what was going on. He spoke clearly to them, particularly about her birth and her father, now long gone. They prayed over these issues, just as they would have done had she been there with them, asking Jesus to go back in time and minister to the hurts and pains, and bring forgiveness for the sins involved, and then they broke any demonic power attached to her birth or her family lines. When they felt a sense of peace, they stopped.

There was an immediate difference, and the twenty-past-three tantrums stopped. The other violent behaviour patterns gradually subsided over the next few months, and Jennifer became not perfect but reasonably normal. She still throws a wobbly now and again, but not that much more than any of the other children in the class, and she can be disciplined for doing so. Further exploration of the family background revealed all sorts of evil influences, and sadly there is not yet complete freedom, and neither will there be until there is repentence or until Jennifer leaves the family environment, but at least the manifestations are being kept under control and other children are safer. There is also some evidence to suggest that there were negative influences over that bit of the city, so there may be even bigger battles to fight.[2]

Quite apart from what it did for Jennifer, the incident helped the teacher. Perhaps without fully realising it she had been in a battle for some time, and she realised that she had been, in 'Ghostbusters' terminology, well and truly 'slimed'. She had been suffering from frequent headaches, and often felt a real sense of heavy oppression over her. She came to realise that her presence with Jennifer, and in particular her attempts to bring Jesus into the classroom with her, had caused her to be the subject of attack herself. Other members of the healing team were able to set her free from this, and her physical symptoms stopped immediately.

Deliverance ministry isn't something for the complete novice, but with a bit of training and experience you can easily begin to pray for children whom you suspect may be troubled in this way. Of course you need some indication that the demonic is involved before you begin praying, but if you suspect anything, it may be that dramatic results will follow your ministry. And as far as we know, no one has yet phoned Child-line to complain that they're being prayed for.

There isn't space here to go into the ways of recognising and discerning the presence of the demonic, and the books mentioned above will give enough details to those who are unfamiliar with this ministry. Children, if present for the ministry, need to be treated no differently from adults in principle, but involving the parents wherever possible (as Jesus did in these two examples) is helpful, as is a full explanation of what is going on. Fear is learnt, and if children see you go into a panic when one of their number reacts dramatically to the presence of the Spirit during a worship time, they will get the message that this is terrifying. But if they see you react calmly and confidently, if you invite them to minister along with you, and if you explain clearly to them what is going on, and above all if you keep smiling all the time and don't get too heavy about it all, they'll soon learn that this is all part of following Jesus and take it in their stride. Children have a tremendous capacity for coping, and it is tragic that so often we infect them with our fear, insecurity and doubt. The whole area of healing and deliverance provides adults with a fresh challenge to obey Jesus' words and become like little children. Let's make sure it doesn't go the other way and we make them become like us.

## Notes

1. Personally we feel that Nigel Wright's *The Fair Face of Evil* (Marshall Pickering: London, 1989) is the most healthy book to have been written recently on spiritual warfare. Those who would take the opposite view can see it taken to extremes in Frank and Ida Mae Hammond, *Pigs in the Parlour* (Impac: Kirkwood, USA, 1973).
2. For information on the whole area of 'Territorial Spirits', see Peter Wagner (ed), *Wrestling with Dark Angels* (Monarch: Tunbridge Wells, 1990), and *Breaking Strongholds in your City* (Monarch: Tunbridge Wells, 1990); John Dawson, *Taking our Cities for God* (Word: Milton Keynes, 1989).

# CHAPTER NINE

# CHILDREN AND THE BIBLE

We've tried to emphasise all along that for us the Bible is the supreme authority in the church, and that the gifts of the Spirit are not to be seen in any way as in competition with Scripture, but rather that the two complement each other as the Spirit illuminates the word and the word provides parameters for the Spirit. The divide in the church between charismatics and evangelicals is so tragic, since we are otherwise so close to each other. How can we teach our children to value both word and Spirit, and live fully in the light of what God *has* said and what he *does* say?

Let's begin by looking at some of the symptoms of neglect of one side or the other of this equation. Everyone is familiar with some of the manifestations of unbridled charismania; you have only to read the Corinthian correspondence to see it in action. The addiction to experience; the lack of spiritual discipline; the selfishness which masquerades as spirituality; the playing down of the importance of a holy lifestyle; empire-building through a divine hotline; lack of submission to leaders; triumphalism which marginalises those experiencing suffering and pain: all these are as common in the church today as they were in Corinth. Indeed, there is special danger in a culture as concerned as ours is with the pursuit of pleasure and experience for those who major on the supernatural gifts of the Spirit. It is very easy to make charismatic Christianity look like yet another New Age trip.

But the other side of the equation, which is less well known but just as nasty, is worth looking at. David Watson describes what he calls 'textualism', quoting Tozer who defined it as 'orthodoxy without the Holy Ghost'. He continues to quote:

children <u>immediate</u> pt capacity
for coping & taking things = their
state (not agonising over things.)

1. Dyt apposeles to children
Anglican — accept as membos / nurture
                                    + discipline
Baptist   not membos til baptizd later.
Free Church — valued bot baptizd later
              (grows into interbode)

2) Impl'ce of obedience / c families / to God

3) children learn image of God from parents
love + obedience.

4) A) Vision of God's work —
   need Word + Spirit (savoir + connaître)
   — must relate to their lives today
   + use of good quality (crafts etc)

— children mustn't take on adults doubts
+ uncertainties — they can be more positive
(adults also naughty — their gossiping etc
children more obvious contrast between
1) reverence 2) restlessness / misdevotion

— children see pictorially
— have a short attention span

Everywhere among conservatives we find persons who are Bible-taught but not Spirit-taught. . . . Truth that is not experienced is no better than error, and may be fully as dangerous. The scribes who sat in Moses' seat were not the victims of error; they were the victims of their failure to experience the truth they taught.

Watson goes on:

Until the Holy Spirit illuminates our dull minds and warms our cold hearts, we do not receive God's revealed truth, no matter how accurately we know the right words and teach them to others.

Richard Wurmbrand once pointed out that in communist prisons he found Christians who knew Bible verses such as 'My grace is sufficient for you', but they found little comfort in these verses alone. It is God's grace that is sufficient for us, not the verse about it.[1]

If charismania was the presenting problem in one book of the Bible, textualism runs throughout many. 'These people come near to me with their mouth and honour me with their lips,' said Isaiah (Is 29:13), 'but their hearts are far from me.' The Psalmist asks the wicked, 'What right have you to recite my laws or take my covenant on your lips? You hate my instruction, and cast my words behind you' (Ps 50:16-17). Jesus picked up verses like these and used them against the Scribes and Pharisees, who epitomised those who love the words of the Law but miss their spirit entirely. Matthew chapter 23 contains devastating criticism of those who were so zealous for the letter of the law that they missed out on the very things the Law taught about the inner life and the fruit of the Spirit.

In other passages we can see Jesus' attack on the self-same shibboleths which the evangelical world is still arguing about today: the use of Sunday (Mt 12:1-14); whether or not 'signs and wonders' can be authenticated empirically (Mt 12:38-39; 16:1-4); what you eat (and perhaps drink or smoke?) (Mt 15:1-20); divorce (Mt 19:1-12), and so much more. It's not that these things don't matter: on the contrary, Jesus' followers must be every bit as holy as the Pharisees, and a lot more besides (Mt 5:20), and they must be as committed to Scripture as those who are renowned for teaching it (Mt 5:17-19). It's just that there are weightier matters to consider too. For all their theology and commitment to the word, the Scribes simply didn't recognise the work of God when they saw it. 'You diligently study the Scriptures because you think that by them you possess eternal life,' said Jesus to the Jewish leaders. 'These are the Scriptures that testify about me, yet you refuse to come to me to have life' (Jn 5:39-40). It requires a particular degree of spiritual deadness to see the power of Jesus and call it the devil at work, but even this was done in the Bible (Mt 12:22-32), and tragically has been done in today's church too. It is interesting to observe the reaction of some of those from certain sections of the church when asked to consider whether some of these criticisms might validly be applied to them. There is often a similar bristling self-righteousness to that with which Jesus was greeted.

The point is, you see, that the sharp cutting edge of the word needs to be sheathed sometimes in the bejewelled scabbard of the Spirit. There are times to go on the offensive and to wield the sword for truth and righteousness, but there are also times to put it away and use love and beauty instead. It seems to be an observable fact in the church that those who are most zealous for the Scriptures can be those who have a hard, cold edge to them which is as profoundly unattractive as it was in Jesus' time. It was the Lawyers and Pharisees who dragged a woman from her lover's bed to Jesus for condemnation, and legally they had every right to do so, but Jesus chose the way of grace instead, no doubt much to their annoyance (Jn 8:1-11). We're not arguing for spiritual laxity, any more than Jesus was spiritually lax on that occasion, but rather for the meeting of law and grace, of righteousness and love. 'Love and faithfulness meet together,' declared the Psalmist. 'Righteousness and peace kiss each other' (Ps 85:10). It is this meeting of faithfulness to Scripture and love given by the Spirit which the church desperately needs.

What does this mean for children's ministry? It means that we must teach not just word and Spirit, but also an understanding of the relationship between them. To clamp down on and denigrate the very spiritual gifts which the New Testament urges us earnestly to desire is an incredible example of doublethink. When the author of the letter to the Ephesians enjoins his readers to be filled with the Spirit so that they overflow in worship and praise, he's not talking to a group of weirdos on the fringe of the church somewhere: this is mainstream biblical Christianity. How can we disobey, teach others to disobey, and then claim to be biblical? It's a nonsense, and our children will see right through it even if we can't. An adage from the early days of renewal is still appropriate: word only – you dry up; Spirit only – you blow up; word and Spirit – you grow up. This balance is essential if children are to grow up avoiding the extremes of pharisaical evangelicalism or loony charismania.

The same is true for those from another branch of the church who would want to edit out of the Bible everything which their 'enlightenment' mindset would consider to be unacceptable, like miracles, healings, resurrection and so on. Children haven't yet become sophisticated enough to play clever adult mindgames. If they read something they treat it either as a fairy story or as truth. If it's truth, they'll begin to ask sooner or later where it is in their own experience and the experience of the church. If they can see it, all well and good, but if not, the credibility of the whole Bible will go out of the window. If on the other hand they're taught that it's a fairy story, they'll simply grow out of it, as thousands of youngsters have this century.

Now you may be thinking that this is a recipe for fundamentalism, and you may quite simply be intellectually unable to accept such a position. Good: so are we. But it's all a question of what you're fundamentalist about, and this leads us onto another point, children and hermeneutics. What that means is that children need to be taught not just that the Bible is there, important and real. They need to be given some clue as to how to understand it. This is obviously a massive subject, and even we can't claim to have a major grasp of it, never mind our children. But we do try to tell them that the subject exists, and to help them begin to understand the questions, if not all the answers.

Many children who are exposed to the Bible imbibe the view (often by default in the absence of anything else to go on) that it dropped out of heaven one day in its finished form. Nowadays most Christians would have an understanding that there was a bit more to it than that, and would be aware of some of the things the theologians spend their time doing with ancient manuscripts and versions. They would also know that there were at least questions about the authorship and dating of some of the books, even if they couldn't find their way through the technical arguments involved. But how often do we bring our children in on this kind of discussion? There seems to be an unarticulated fear lurking around the minds of leaders that biblical criticism and interpretation is X-rated stuff for adults only. Why this fear? Because many of them were brought up, either as children or as new adult Christians, with the same naive oblivion to these questions which we've already mentioned. When they first encountered them the shock was great, and they've responded often by putting all such things on one side as too intellectually difficult and too threatening to the belief that 'this is the word of the Lord'. So to expose mere children to such unsettling questions will do them irreparable harm.

Is it possible to do degree-level theology with five-year-olds? Of course it is. It's just a case of being willing to say that we don't know sometimes. John believes fervently in three Isaiahs, not, as he was once told by an angry speaker at Spring Harvest, because he doesn't believe in the supernatural power of God to predict the future (he does), but because he really couldn't see the point of God doing it when the message he wanted them to hear in a hundred years' time was exactly the opposite of the one they needed now. So why not send a different prophet later? His theological study has confirmed him in this view many times over, and he feels perfectly happy about it. So why not tell the children that? What harm will it do to explain to them that the book they're reading from *probably* came from three different people, but got put together later into one book? For most of them this will actually be a matter of profound indifference, but that's not a reason to leave it out. One day they'll have to face it, and it can be very painful for them.

It wasn't until his mid-twenties at theological college that John had to re-examine all his fundamentalist presuppositions, and he could easily have gone under as the foundations of his faith crumbled. He had been taught, either specifically or tacitly, that it mattered that Isaiah wrote Isaiah, or that Daniel dates from the sixth century, or that the Gospels do tell the same story really. To prepare children for this kind of awareness by showing that there are questions and uncertainties but that they're not that crucial is a vital work. It isn't an undermining of the supreme authority of the Bible: it's just reality.

In the past we were taught that the Bible was authoritative

because it was the Word of God and all that; we're proposing a different way. For children the Bible is authoritative if they see their parents and leaders loving it, valuing it, using it and obeying it. Questions about who actually wrote it are secondary. We can be unclear or agnostic about the authorship of Ephesians, and we can explain that fact to our children, but the real issue is whether or not we live it out. Do we expect obedience and manage to get it without exasperation (theirs, not ours)? Do we know what it means to be filled with the Spirit, clothed in the armour, and living as children of the light? You see it's not what we believe about the Bible which is crucial: that's open to debate. It's whether or not we respect and obey it which counts as far as our children are concerned.

Now of course this approach may sound dangerously liberal to some, or suspiciously like wanting to have our cake and eat it to others. How can we possibly be so certain about the reality of the supernatural on the one hand and yet be so agnostic about the text on the other? Aren't we trying to be liberal and fundamentalist at the same time, and won't that confuse our children beyond their ability to cope? No, and the reason is this: some things we can't know, so we don't worry too much about them, but some things we can, so we'll go for them. One day John will meet Isaiah(s) and find out whether he or his Spring Harvest ranter was right. One day he'll be able to say to St Paul, 'Come on, tell me the truth: Did you do Ephesians or not? Give it to me straight; I can take it.' He's looking forward to that day, but for now we're quite honestly not that bothered. But speaking in tongues? Yes, it's real, here and now; St Paul (if he did write 1 Corinthians) would love us all to do it, so here we go. See the difference? It's about sorting out the intellectual questions from the practical ones. It's about obedience. And with children it's about not letting them get the impression things are sewn up when we really can't be that sure, but neither letting them miss out on what God the Holy Spirit has got for them.

So how might this work out in practice? We'll end this chapter with four brief headings, under each of which will be an actual case study of something we've done to work out these principles.

## 1. Socialising

This is a term which refers to the fact that we learn as much by being with the right people as we do from studying the right material. Medical students, for example, tend to behave in certain ways because they've learnt to do so by being with other medical students. This is a recognised sociological phenomenon, and it applies all over the place, from senior common rooms to ante-natal clinics. So we can use it to our (and the childrens' advantage) by seeking deliberately to create a climate where the Bible is valued and used. As soon as they enter our six-to-elevens group, children are presented with a *Good News Bible* and a set of Bible reading notes appropriate to their age. There is from time to time teaching about regular Bible reading, but far more often there is just the tacit assumption that as Christians we will read it, so we talk about what people have been reading this week, how God has spoken to them, and so on. The socialisation seems to do as much good as the more direct teaching does.

## 2. Memorising

We believe it is important to learn biblical verses off by heart, but we've found that this can be transformed from a dull exercise into a living encounter with God by personalising what the children remember. We mentioned in chapter four Steve's photo held securely in the hands of God. Another example of this same thing in action was a picture of a soldier in armour, again drawn by a talented artist, with the words 'Steve – put on all the armour that God gives you' written colourfully across it. This too became a treasured bedroom ornament which provided a reminder each morning.

This same approach can be used to make the words of the Bible more accessible to youngsters. 'Go throughout the whole world and preach the gospel to all mankind' is a big challenge by anyone's standards, but if it can be altered slightly to read 'Go throughout Grange Farm School and preach the gospel' it immediately becomes something much more within reach. After all, it's good to begin small: they can move on to the rest of the world once they've learnt to cross the road.

Another tremendously powerful aid to memorising is the use of Scripture songs. There is a vast quantity of material by Ishmael and others which the children love to sing, which is simple enough to be picked up and learnt quickly, and which stay in the children's heads throughout the week, thus constantly feeding them with God's word. Not only this; there are even songs like 'Have you got an appetite?' which, rather than just being a verse from the Bible, is about the value of feeding on the Bible. Children love these songs, and they really do help Scripture to get in and stay in. And if there isn't a song for the particular verse you're wanting to use, why not write your own? You'd be amazed at how easy it can be; many parents have done the same thing instinctively with young children.

## 3. Studying

An interesting series, designed to introduce children to criticism and hermeneutics, began by the leaders finding examples of different types of literature from everyday life. One brought a thank-you letter to Aunty Mabel for the lovely scarf, another read a nursery rhyme; there were also a section from a history book and a bit of the Highway Code, and so on. As they were read out, the children had to identify what type of writing they were.

Then followed some teaching about the inappropriateness of confusing different types and using them for the wrong purpose: thanking Aunty Mabel by telling her not to overtake near a humpback bridge, or asking exactly *when* the cow had jumped over the moon, and how it had managed such an incredible feat of aerodynamics. As you can imagine, this was great fun.

But it led on to a serious discussion, illustrated from different parts of the Bible, about the need to be every bit as discerning with what we read. We can get into just as much of a mess if we misunderstand how the different *genres* in the Bible work, and what exactly they're meant to tell us. This was then applied practically with some work on how we might respond to different styles: we'd obey commands, worship through poetic passages, and so on. Thus the children were introduced, in a fun and accessible way, to some teaching which many adults have never mastered!

## 4. Applying

While we do intend everything we do with the Bible to be

applicable to real life, we can still have sessions where we particularly work on this. The children's themes will often tie in with those of the adult teaching series, although the level of application will obviously be different. A year or so ago John felt that God was telling him to preach through the book of Haggai. The church was at a stage where it needed consciously to switch from tinkering with its own internal structures and turn inside out to make outreach the priority, to stop making home-improvements in our panelled houses and start building the Temple of the Lord. So the children too studied Haggai during this period, at their own level.

First of all there was some background teaching which told the children that this wasn't just a story, it was about a real person who lived at a real time in a real place. What would it have been like to have lived then? All sorts of background information was taught in a way which helped the children to step in their imagination into the prophet's world. The next session simply made the point that in a time when everyone was very busy on their own interests, Haggai heard God. This allowed a recap on how we hear God (you see it, you read it, you feel it, you know it, you say it), plus some teaching on the fact that if we are going to hear God speaking to us we need to slow down and give him space and time. Quite naturally a practical session followed, where the Spirit came and the children listened and shared prophetic words and pictures.

Next week we talked about obedience: Haggai's to God, and the people's to Haggai. And so it went on. Critical questions were not ignored, the work of the Spirit was built in, and the teaching was applied to the children's own personal lives. This kind of approach, which takes seriously intellect and experience, is not impossible with young children; it just means that the leaders have to be a bit more theologically clued up and imaginative. But then, as we'll go on to say in the next chapter, children's work is never the easy option!

## Notes

1. David Watson, *Discipleship* (Hodder and Stoughton: London, 1981), p 145.

CHAPTER TEN

# THE LEADER

It so happened in our last church that we had two crises at the same time (that was a good week, with only two). The first was that we urgently needed more people to count the collection after services, and the second was that there was no one to look after the babies and toddlers in the crèche. The leadership made a policy decision that we could not ask just anyone to count money: they had to be people we knew and trusted, and whose integrity and honesty was beyond question. We would personally approach people whom we had listed as fitting the bill. At the same time we made a general appeal at our Sunday services for anyone who could help with the children to have a word afterwards.

What we had done dawned on us fairly quickly. We had acted as though money was more important than children. Anyone would do for them, but money had to be handled by the 'right' people, lest anything should go wrong. This attitude pervades much of the church. Consider, for example, the human and physical geography of your church life. Could it be that the adults, at one end of the scale, will be in the best room, with the best musicians and the best speaker, while at the other end the babies will be tucked away in a broom cupboard somewhere, presided over by a few women or teenagers who have been pressganged into doing a shift on the rota?

This attitude also shows itself when church leaders and people alike regard work with children as a kind of poor relation. It is often seen as a temporary stage through which people must pass before they are allowed to do something significant in the church. When Chris became a Christian at the age of fourteen she was immediately sent off to lead a Pathfinder Group (for tens to

107

fourteens). This model assumes that even a brand new Christian will have all that is needed to work with youngsters, although they will hopefully learn enough in the process so that one day they will be able to graduate and lead a homegroup for adults, or something equally important. While God may, of course, call us to different areas of ministry as we travel on in our Christian pilgrimage, we need children's workers who will see their ministry as a proper ministry, and not just a stepping-stone to greater things. We wouldn't of course want to ban teenagers or new Christians from children's work, but we would want them to work alongside leaders who were mature both in age and Christian discipleship.

So what sort of people might be able to lead children into things of the Spirit? Let's begin negatively by looking at the sorts of attitudes which won't help.

First of all, a belief that the spiritual gifts died out at the end of the apostolic age and are therefore not for the church today might just be a bit of a hindrance in leading children into their use. The view that gifts were a bit like the choke on your car, useful for getting you going from cold, but thereafter to be pushed in and forgotten, leads to the conclusion that all so-called manifestations of the Spirit nowadays are spurious or even satanic counterfeits. Understandably, no one would want to lead children, or anyone else, into that sort of thing. Similarly, the view that the so-called 'supernatural' gifts are somewhat overrated, and we ought to be putting our energy not into tongues and prophecy but into other biblical ministries like flower-arranging, will militate against children entering into the full inheritance of the Spirit which is theirs (ie tongues *and* flower-arranging). Leaders must be committed to an understanding of the Spirit which involves the full range of his activities in the church.

There is also a common attitude that the things of the Spirit are rather like condoms: they have their right and proper use, and we personally have no problem with that, but we certainly wouldn't mention them to those who are too young. They'll be able to find out about things like that all in good time, when they're more grown up, and any questions now are gently deflected in a slightly embarrassed manner.

And thirdly, there are those who have no theological objections as such to charismatic renewal; it's just that it scares them half to death, either because they have fantasies about what goes on in charismatic churches or because they have seen what goes on in

charismatic churches or because they have seen what goes on in
charismatic churches! A leader suffering in this way will find it
difficult to put the subject across convincingly, and without
communicating his own terror.

It is worth considering these attitudes, because it is sometimes the
case in churches which are moving into charismatic renewal that
those who are most unhappy with the new direction and its manifestations are to be found in the Sunday school. As the services get more
ravey, the guitars more loud, the spiritual gifts more frequent and the
sermons more challenging, those who are threatened by this may
gravitate to the Sunday school where it is safe. They have their own
little empire where they can continue to teach nice Bible stories and
keep the experience of God at arm's length. If there is a Sunday in
the month when the Sunday school is not functioning and the whole
church worships together, they stay away, claiming the need for 'a
day off', and their absence from other activities such as fellowship
groups is striking. Thus they can not only escape from the Spirit
themselves, but also model non-involvement to the children in their
care, effectively steering them out of the main flow of the church and
into a calm spiritual backwater.

If this is a problem for you it may need to be tackled head-on by
the church leadership. People may need to be gently challenged,
their fears and hesitations listened to, and their concerns treated
seriously, while at the same time they need to know that this is the
direction the church is going in, and if they can't lead children
confidently in it, perhaps they would be better off counting the
collection. This is a sensitive matter, but it does need confronting
if we are to avoid creating a great chasm between the children and
the rest of the church. If the overall leader of the children's ministry
wants a particular ethos to pervade the work, they will find it
helpful to spell out from day one where they are going and what
will be required of leaders.

Anyone who wants to join our team is not immediately
welcomed with open arms: they are first told about the vision for
the work (as set out in chapter four) and asked if they can happily
commit themselves at that level. They are asked at which of the
other Sunday services they will worship regularly: that's also part
of the commitment. We try to help them see that along with the
privilege of leadership goes responsibility, and that we want a

commitment to remain involved for a period of time which, while not a life-sentence, will give them enough time to work through the problems they may face initially. They are then given time to go away and pray and think through their calling, so that there is no sense of rush or pressure, and if they conclude that it could be right for them they are invited to work for a few months on a probationary basis, after which there will be a review on both sides. So we do try to spell out very clearly what the commitment means: people won't always understand or hear what is being said, but later on we are able to say, 'Don't say I didn't warn you!' It's not that we're looking for fully competent and experienced leaders, but we do want those who are happy to be trained in this ethos and model.

We also try to be as careful about the end of their ministry as we are about the beginning. People will have to leave your team for all sorts of reasons, so we spell out the rules for that too. We ask for a term's notice, so that we have time to seek replacements for them (and that is *our* responsibility, not *theirs*), and so that new people can work alongside them for a while to settle them in. We ask that all the leaders of a particular sub-group do not give up at once, but stagger their going to provide continuity for the children in their care, and we do try to ensure that when people leave they move on to another area of ministry and don't just flop out and do nothing. We'll try to see they join another home-group too.

Ongoing envisioning and training is needed: our children and youth workers meet weekly as a homegroup, and no one who is not a part of that group is allowed to lead on Sundays. As well as programme-planning, the group concentrates on overall policy and vision, prayer and worship, and personal growth in discipleship. In addition, members of the team are encouraged (and paid!) to attend outside training events, such as the annual Charismatic Children's Leaders' Conference, run by the Glorie Company. While it has been necessary on a couple of occasions to lay down the law as suggested above, it has been far more our experience that within this intimate and caring environment those with hesitations about the Spirit have been led on to a much more confident place. We must at all costs, though, make sure that there is 'no hiding-place' from the Spirit among the children's work of our churches.

So what sort of positive characteristics do we want our leaders to have? Four main qualifications seem important: we'll look at each in turn.

## 1. Spiritually open

First of all, we need leaders who are open to the Spirit themselves, and who have a heart to see children moving in the same way. We need to break free of the traditional model of children's work which sees it as an easy option for the spiritually not-quite-there. Instead, we need those who will realise that it can be much more demanding than they'd ever dreamed, but are willing to rise to the challenge. No longer is it a glorified baby-sitting service so that the adults can get on uninterrupted with the real thing over in the church. We need those who will understand that they have a spiritual ministry which is part of the whole continuum of disciple-making. We need crèche workers who will pray over the babies they are soothing; toddlers' group leaders who will talk naturally about and to Jesus in the company of the youngsters with whom they're playing, and so on. It's never too early to begin, and we need to challenge the mentality of some Christians who feel they can help with the tinies because they're not spiritual enough for anything more advanced.

## 2. Spiritually ahead

Secondly, we need leaders who are ahead of the children spiritually, but who are also at the same time willing to learn from them. We've already mentioned the fact that young children are gloriously free from our adult hang-ups about the supernatural, and so can advance quickly in the things of the Spirit if they are led in the right way. Many of them can put adult Christians to shame in their levels of faith and expectancy. But conversely they can be held back by leaders who don't believe (or don't want to believe) they can cope. In the early days it was common in our team homegroup to hear leaders protesting that 'the children won't be able to cope with . . .' praying aloud, speaking in tongues or whatever. What they actually meant was, 'I won't cope!' Another common ploy was to plead age: one lot of leaders would say that all this was fine for the *older* children, who could cope, but ours are much too young, while at the same time the others were saying that theirs were too old for this stuff and we ought to restrict it to the *younger* group. A team leader who spots this attitude and lovingly confronts it, and who then goes on to show just how easily the children *will* cope in practice, whatever their age, can achieve much for the growth not only of the children but also the adults as well. But in the absence of such a team leader these beliefs can go unchallenged and gain general acceptance, so that children are robbed of spiritual experience with which they would be more than happy. This loss of nerve must be attacked, or else it will rule the roost most destructively.

Another dangerous attitude is one which is in favour of leading the ministry in a particular direction, but would rather someone else did the dirty work for them. Part of our job in the past was to lead teams visiting other churches for faith-sharing weekends, and it was amazing how often we were brought in to do various kinds of hatchet-jobs which the church leaders couldn't face doing themselves. By all means invite others to give input to your children's work, but only if you are all willing to do lots of ground work before they come, and then pick up what they've brought and carry on in the same direction.

A team leader may have to deal with the sense of threat which team members may experience as they realise that they never did any of this with their own children. They can be easily made to feel inferior, or failures, as they come to realise how much more spiritually aware their children could have been if they had known about this years ago. It may feel too late now to do anything about it, especially if their children have now ceased to live as Christians. The real problem is that they'll very rarely admit this sense of shame and guilt. If they did, there could be ministry to them, and a setting free from guilt and regrets (after all, that is what the gospel is about). But it is far more common for this guilt to be buried, and rationalised with the feeling that it isn't right to give children this kind of spiritual experience just because mine didn't get it. Children's work can be held up quite seriously if this attitude pervades, and again a sensitive team leader will need to do some gentle surgery to expose feelings about one's own past to the healing love of the group and of the Lord.

At the same time as being ahead and willing to lead the children, though, leaders must be willing to learn from the children they're there to teach. Jesus once used a child as a visual aid, telling his disciples,'Unless you change and become like little children, you will never enter the kingdom of heaven. Therefore, whoever humbles himself like this child is the greatest in the kingdom of heaven' (Mt 18:3-4). While the leaders need to be ahead, they must not be superior and patronising to children, and must be open to great spiritual insight coming through them. The humility to learn from those who will at times put us to shame is a kingdom characteristic essential in children's leaders.

Maybe a good picture would be walking a dog. Although neither of us has any great expertise in this area (John fervently believes that all animals should be where the good Lord intended them to be: in zoos), we have nevertheless picked up one crucial understanding: it is quite difficult to *push* a dog along on a lead. In fact, no matter how hard you try, you can't get it to go anywhere by standing behind and pushing: the knack is to go out in front and pull. In the same way you won't get children into the gifts of the Spirit by standing behind them: you've got to go out in front first. That is, after all, what 'leading' means. But, to continue the canine analogy, there will be times when your enthusiastic pet will suddenly get onto the scent of something and really go for it. You will find yourself being pulled along and, depending on the size and make of the dog in question, you may find it quite hard to resist. You can't push children into spiritual experience, but you can pull them, and you must be ready for those times when they'll end up pulling you.

## 3. Spiritually Committed

Thirdly, we need children's leaders who are called and committed to the task. The whole work of the church should in fact be staffed by those people who have a sense of calling, but this is especially important when it comes to those areas which are to do with the formation of Christian character and discipleship. By their commitment, leaders will model both the commitment of our faithful God to us, and also the commitment to the body of Christ which the true disciple will exhibit. At a time in our society when there is little commitment to anything at all, and when many parents will attend worship only when they've nothing more exciting to do, there is much which models to children those hop-and-a-catch attitudes to church and to Christ himself which are so destructive of true discipleship.

The problem with modelling commitment as a clergy family is that people can write us off by saying, 'Well of course you're paid to be there!' Our children need other role-models, and plenty of them, in whom they can see commitment to the kingdom of God as an all-consuming passion which comes at the very top of the list of priorities. Our boys know, and they have known for years, that they simply are not allowed to take part in sporting or uniformed group activities which conflict with Sunday worship. So far there is not a hint of resentment about this; they agree wholeheartedly with us that Jesus must come first, and that their other activities must make way for him. How this will change as time goes by remains to be seen, but we suspect that the secret is to agree with them as early as possible that this is the policy, and to stick to it without a hint of vacillation. They'd no more expect to do something other than worship on a Sunday morning than they would expect to do something other than go to school on a Monday: it's simply not an option. They don't respond to friends who do play football or whatever with jealousy; they feel sorry that they haven't got Jesus and therefore something better to do. We've seen so many young disciples diverted from their Christian commitment by their sporting or musical skills that we don't want to run that risk with ours, and they understand and would not want us to. This attitude is a choice of will which has nothing to do with us being 'professional' Christians; any family could adopt it if they felt it important enough.

Sadly, though, the Enemy has duped many Christian parents into colluding with him as he tries to wreck children's spiritual lives. We were recently stunned to hear a speaker, addressing Christians, say that for most parents it's more important that our children get a good job than that they walk with the Lord. This is so obviously true as we look around our churches and see parents fuelling their children's ambitions in the sporting, musical, dramatic or academic arenas at the expense of their spiritual growth. Polly Toynbee, writing from a secular point of view, attacks the commonly-held view that we must do all we can to stimulate our children and make life fun for them:

The anxious new parent these days from the earliest years will feel the pressing need to occupy every moment of their toddlers' lives with stimulation and entertainment. . . . The swimming classes, the Tumble Tots, the dancing lessons and Suzuki method violin, the Saturday morning French club, ballet and tap and the drama workshops. Wonderful, yes. But what are we saying to our kids? Life is an endless cycle of pleasure designed just for you? Everything and everyone is bent on your enjoyment, for it is the only purpose of our lives?[1]

Clearly that is not a good message to give, since they'll discover only too soon that it simply isn't true. It's also common to see parents living out through their children the childhood they wish they'd had, as they move heaven and earth to get them to various other activites while worship and fellowship go by the board. We have so much to learn about finding our fulfilment in following Jesus, and finding our security and significance in his love. The Enemy will do all he can to dilute Christian commitment among adults and children alike, and he is not averse to using good things to keep us from the best thing: it is our conviction that we need to fight him, not help him.

Another reason why we suspect our boys are happy with this level of commitment is that they see it modelled in us. There are all sorts of ways we'd love to spend Sundays, but for the sake of the kingdom we chose to sacrifice them when we responded to God's call to ministry. We have not reached the full potential which might have been ours as, for example, golfers, but we count it a privilege to have ditched that possibility for the sake of the kingdom, and our hope and prayer is that our boys will feel the same about their sacrifices. They would rather Dad didn't have to take five services on a Sunday, of course, but they fully understand why he has chosen to. Children will spot half-heartedness a mile off, and their eyesight will get even sharper as they grow older. Leaders who are not totally committed to the kingdom and the church will lose credibility among children who are, and will model a take-it-or-leave-it attitude to those who are not.

Every year the City of Coventry holds a fun-run which raises thousands of pounds for charity and is a thoroughly good thing – except that it begins while our Sunday morning service is on. In spite of repeated letters to the organisers (to which we've never even had a reply), it has not been moved to allow Christians who put worship first to take part. So we don't: we worship God instead. Some regard our attitude as stick-in-the-mud and spoil-sport, but we have thought about what it will say to our children if we make the exception. It'll tell them that God comes at number two in the list of priorities, and that simply isn't a message we want to give. God won't be fitted in at our convenience when we've nothing better to do; he demands the first place in everything. Our leaders need to understand and model this attitude if we are to put up a united front against these subtle forces.

## 4. Spiritual heroes

It is a characteristic of children, and one which grows as they do, that they need heroes. There are so many likely contenders in the world around, and they change with alarming frequency. As we write, Arnie Schwarzenegger, Leonardo and his pizza-loving chelonian pals, Bart Simpson, Super Mario and Hulk Hogan seem to be on the way out, and Michael Jordan has just retired. By the time you finally get to read this there'll be no telling who's the current favourite, and you'll be thinking how quaint and nostalgic this paragraph is, and who was Michael Jordan anyway? But the fact is that many of these heroes are modelling the very opposite of Christian virtues, or at best attitudes to life which leave God out altogether. Where are all the Christian heroes? Wonderful though he may be to the sixties' generation, Cliff doesn't cut much ice with our kids. Simon Mayo is doing a good job, and the appearance of Roy Castle at Spring Harvest left a deep impression on many of the youngsters in our party, but there aren't many of that calibre. And the least likely object of this type of adulation will be your vicar! If Christians don't fill the need which youngsters have for heroes, there are plenty of others ready to come and take their place. Is it too much to expect that some of your children's work leaders could fit the bill?

As we write, our Steve has just been picked for the school football first team. He's been after this for a long time, slowly working his way towards it, and today he made it! As John interrupted his typing of this to pick him up from the practice and drive him home, he asked Steve if he had any heroes. Expecting some great footballing superstar to be top of the list (he could remember worshipping Danny Blanchflower himself in the past), John was surprised but gratified when without hesitation the answer came back: 'Ishmael'. If our leaders are exciting people, living out an exciting faith with a wholehearted commitment, children can't help but look up to them. Steve already believes he has a calling to work with children. He clearly has gifting in that direction which is already apparent, and this call has been mediated through two people whom he respects and values highly who work in this area: Ishmael and his mum. Gifted leaders give birth to more gifted leaders, just as mediocre ones create mediocrity among their protégés.

It is also worth mentioning the fact here that children need same-sex heroes. Sunday schools are often staffed by women, and while it may be the case occasionally that they do provide good role-modelling, they can only possibly do so for the girls. We need to see the vital importance of attracting men into children's ministry alongside women, and in particular men who are not like old women! This isn't a matter of sexism, it's just a matter of fact. Boys need men to look up to, and our children's work needs to have some guts to it if we are to attract butch men who will in turn attract boys and model virile Christianity to them.

Is all this too idealistic? Maybe you're left feeling that your set-up is so hopelessly unlike these ideals that you might as well give up now. If you are, we know just how you feel because that's what ours has always been like when we've begun. It isn't so much that people are doing a bad job: more often it's just an uninformed and un-thought-out job. So the first ingredient which needs to be injected is some vision. The team leader, who will hopefully have been envisioned by God for the task, must begin to infect others with this vision, and with his or her enthusiasm for it. If God has truly called you to leadership, and given you a vision to work with, he will not have called you in isolation: he will also have been at work in the hearts of others. Our experience, which was more or less the same in each of our different parishes, was that three things began to happen as the vision was spread around.

The first is that people will get out of the way. Sometimes this is a painful and negative experience for all concerned, but more often it is with a sigh of relief that some who have ministered faithfully for years if not decades will hand on the baton to the next phase of leadership. They had thought that children's work was a life-sentence, but now they find they can be released into something new. It seems to be the case that those who go gladly will find their way into another area of ministry and become contented there, while those who try to hang on when God is telling them it's time to go will become the malcontents who lose all sense of Christian identity along with their job title. It is the fault of the church that they have been allowed to find their status in their job, and it is terribly sad when they go angrily and bitterly, feeling that they no longer have a place in the church now that 'their' job has been taken away from them. This ought to be the exception, though, and your call will be confirmed to you as you see the way opening up before you.

The second thing to happen, and perhaps the rarest, is that some of the existing team will grasp your vision and run with it. God's work in their hearts will have been to cause discontent, as they have become more and more unhappy with the way things are while not really knowing what on earth to do about it. God will have been forming questions in their minds, and they will be ready and enthusiastic when you come along with some answers. Rather than wanting to leave the team, they will be hungry to learn from the new leader, although at times they will feel a bit insecure and want to revert to the older, safer ways. They may need reminding of the discontent they feel, but in a way which helps them to understand that you are building on the past, not writing it off and reversing it.

Thirdly, God will have been at work in others putting on their hearts a call to join you in your new ministry. It may be rather inchoate at present, but like the sheep of Jesus' analogy they will hear your voice and respond by following you. In particular, you will begin to identify those who are still quite young but who may have a ministry with children awaiting them. Your structures need to be capable of including them in appropriate ways which will allow them to experience ministry and also to receive further training and envisioning from you.

It has never been easy rounding up a new team of workers, but it has never been impossible either. If you find yourself truly alone, with no evidence that God is working on others alongside you, it might be right to begin to ask questions about your own call, whether its time has yet come, or whether it might be a call to work alongside others for a˙ while, rather than to take on overall leadership. If God really wants your children's ministry to go places, he'll have made sure he sets it up for you. So begin to pray first of all for a vision, secondly for the space to work it out, and thirdly for those who will work with you. Realise that it'll take time to mould a team together, so build for yourselves a small-steps programme. Rejoice over minor triumphs, reflect on and learn from major disasters, and build one another up in love. You and the Spirit between you can make a pretty good team!

**Notes**

1.   Polly Toynbee, article in the *Radio Times* (12-18 March 1994).

# CHAPTER ELEVEN

# CHILDREN AND THE CHURCH

We began this book by talking about partnership. Now we must return to the subject, because although the children's ministry can have an important effect in leading youngsters into the things of the Spirit, it doesn't happen in isolation. Our Steve has just learnt in his science lessons about the 'fire triangle'. For something to burn there needs to be three ingredients: fuel, oxygen and heat. Take any one of them away, and the fire can't keep going. This is a picture of the fire of God's Spirit: there is in fact a three-way partnership between the children's work, the church as a whole and the human family. If one of these is closed to the work of the Spirit, the children's experience will die down and merely smoulder when we really want them to be well and truly on fire for the Lord.

This chapter is about the church side of this relationship. We have known churches where the children's work was going great guns, but the church itself had a positively medieval attitude towards it. However good the time children spend in their own groups, they will pick up clear messages from the time they spend with the whole church. How can we make these messages positive rather than negative? The answer has to do with rights and responsibilities.

In 1989 the Children's Act became law in Britain. Into a climate of growing awareness (if not necessarily growing incidence) of all kinds of child abuse, this new legislation sought to recognise that children are people too, and they have rights just as much as any adult. At the time this seemed a very positive step, but now we are increasingly seeing what one journalist calls 'the curious philosophy behind it, which is now suddenly coming home to roost'. Commenting on the sharp rise in false accusations aimed by children at their teachers, she asks, 'What on earth did we mean when we decided children should in effect be treated as if they were adults, with full rights? . . . What do we mean by rights for those too young to take adult responsibility?'[1] Many have likened oppressed and abused children to other oppressed minority groups in society, but there is one major difference. If one is a woman, or black, one is fairly likely to remain so for the rest of one's life. The oppressors are presumably not women or black, and therefore have no idea how it feels, hence the oppression. But children are different. Being a child is a temporary phase, which all of us adults have been through. Any attempt to deal with children's rights must be different.

We mention this because there is much discussion about the 'rights' of children as members of churches. In the past there has been much abuse: babies who so much as burped during the service were glared at, there were stewards or churchwardens ready to ask parents to control their noisy offspring or even to remove them. Children who did stay were ignored, or patronised with a two minute 'children's address'. Many young families were frightened away from church altogether, as the number of congregations nowadays with no one under sixty shows.

But now it's all different. Children are, as we've said, the church of today, and they have rights, just as any member does. They have the right to have their say in a service, even if it is at a quiet moment and even if it does disrupt the worship of a couple of hundred other people. They have the right to wander about without restraint, to wrap themselves round the minister's leg while he's preaching, to swing from the altar-cloth and bring communion vessels down on their heads while their parents smile benignly from their seats, celebrating their children's freedom and the wonderful church's relaxed attitude towards them. They have the right to a little bit of their parents' communion bread, even though the discipline of the church says that they're not old enough to have been through whatever it is that allows them to receive. Meanwhile many older people, who no longer feel the church is giving them their rights to a reverent and well-managed service, use their right to stay away instead.

Something has gone wrong, as any teacher will tell you. The pendulum has swung too far, and the church, as well as the state, is confused as to how to behave. Just what are children's rights, and how do they work within the church family?

The simple answer, surely, is that they have the right to a church which treats them as God would, and just as their human parents should: we've already argued this point in chapter three. We'll suggest six ways in which this right must be worked out, and then move on to the other side of the coin, their responsibilities.

## 1. The right to be understood

We've argued already that the children in our care are to be helped to grow in the fruit and gifts of the Spirit, to become more and more aware of their inheritance as children of God, and to be protected against the forces which would teach them to devalue that inheritance and drag them away from it. But how do children grow? We've said that we want to provide for them both intellectual information about, and practical experience of God, but in order to avoid treating them inappropriately we need to have some understanding of their psychology and spirituality. By learning about their needs, we may be in a better position to lead them on.

Two important studies of this subject have been done by John Westerhoff[2] and James Fowler.[3] As you might expect with scholarly studies they reach different conclusions, but they agree in saying that children develop their faith through different stages. A useful summary of their work can be found in an Anglican General Synod report entitled *Children in the Way*,[4] but it will be worth outlining it even more briefly here, in order to see how it fits with our philosophy of discipling children.

Westerhoff's model is the simpler, with four stages. Children begin, he claims, with an 'experienced faith', based not on what we tell them about Christianity but on how adults are as Christians with their children. They sense, explore, observe and copy the stimuli around them, and experience through interaction. Next comes the stage of 'affiliative faith'. Here belonging is important, and membership of a community of faith which consciously identifies itself as such is vital. The child joins in the activities of the community, listens to its stories, and shares something of the awe and mystery which hold the community together. The child needs to be accepted and to feel a sense of togetherness, and will take on board much that a significant and trusted leader gives to them, often in the context of a peer group which is also trusted.

The child then enters a 'searching faith' phase, where he or she will question, experiment, look at other points of view, and finally arrive at a faith which works because it makes sense to them, rather than because someone else has taught them to believe it. This in turn leads to an 'owned faith' which is a mature holding together of different approaches (while maintaining a commitment to one) along with a new appreciation of the myth, symbolism and ritual of the church. Arriving here (and this arrival is what Westerhoff calls 'conversion') enables the Christian to make a stand for his or her faith, even when doing so alienates them to some degree from the community in which they have grown up.

Fowler's analysis of the same journey is more complex and uses even longer words, but the main ideas are not incompatible with Westerhoff's. His first stage, the 'primal' phase of seeing parents as 'superordinate power and wisdom' (that means they're like God, as we mentioned in chapter three) soon gives way to the 'intuitive-projective', where the child moves to a joining in with the stories, symbols and rituals of the faith. Then he moves on to the third stage of 'mythic-literal' faith where the stories and rules of the family are valued, even though they don't provide a particularly coherent meaning for life. Next comes the 'synthetic-conventional' phase, where some of these elements are put together with the child's own life-experience in the search for an overall meaning. The fifth stage is that of 'individuative-reflective' faith, where a conscious awareness of having a belief system which is different from that of others is developed, an awareness which is capable of articulation in abstract terms.

This stage eventually gives way to the next – that of 'paradoxical-consolidative' faith. What happens here is that many opposing viewpoints are examined fully for the first time, and held in tension with others, until finally the pilgrim arrives at the climactic seventh 'universalising' stage, where (and here only a direct quotation will do) 'coherence gives a new simplicity centred on "a oneness beyond but inclusive of the manyness of Being"'![5] One wonders whether there is then a graduation to a whole new level, where begins the eternal and unending quest for the word 'manyness' in a self-respecting English dictionary.

One point needs to be made to do justice to both Westerhoff and Fowler: although we have used the term 'child' to describe the plucky traveller through these sinister-sounding regions, the fact is that age doesn't really come into it all that much. Many adults have never progressed in their faith past the first couple of stages, while some children race through as far as their intellectual capacities will carry them. So it is difficult to say that a child *ought* to have got somewhere by a particular age: it just depends.

Clearly this research is very clever, but the chances are that most of the leaders in your children's ministry will not find it life-changing to any high degree. Is it possible to distil out some helpful and jargon-free principles which can make our discipling of children more effective?

First of all, both writers agree that faith is a growing, dynamic thing rather than something you haven't got one minute but acquire the next. And while intellectual growth doesn't guarantee spiritual maturity, the lack of it can certainly limit it. A young child simply hasn't got the mental equipment to weigh up opposing views on the authorship and date of the book of Daniel, but he'll love the bit about the lions because he saw one once in the zoo. This speaks to the anxiety we mentioned over indoctrination: young children will just need to be told things.

Secondly, there is agreement over the need for youngsters to make the faith and belief their own. A period of questioning and indeed of letting go of some things is an important part of the acquisition of mature faith. How much more helpful it is, then, for the child to have experiences of God as well as information about him to weigh up. It is probably at this stage that most youngsters give up on the church, as they examine and test what they've been told, only to find that there is no empirical evidence for any of it in their own lives or in the life of their church. Knowing that Jesus was supposed to have healed sick people must inevitably raise sooner or later questions about whether he still does. That question is easier to answer positively if you've seen him do it, or felt him do it to you!

Thirdly, the need throughout the process for an accepting and nurturing community is paramount, and we will examine this more closely in due course as we try to discover to what kind of church community children have 'the right'. But before we leave them, we have a final reflection on Westerhoff and Fowler.

They clearly do have things of value to teach us, even if we can't pronounce them. We're not so sure, however, about the so-called arrivals at the final stage which each describes. We prefer to think of a mature Christian as one who will make a stand for the truth of the faith, rather than as one who has discovered their place in the manyness of Being, but then we're just old-fashioned. But if maturity is, as seems to be implied, a loss of the child-like innocence which just takes God at his word and obeys him, then surely we've got it rather on its head. Jesus told his disciples that they needed to go back a few stages when they thought they'd arrived. Of course a child's faith needs to grow to a level of sophistication beyond that which they could manage when they first joined the crèche, but we'd want to resist any suggestion that maturity is about becoming cleverer than God, and learning to sit in judgement over his word. The gospel way is that while the adults have much to teach children, they have even more to learn from them.

## 2. The right to be accepted

There is no doubt that children need an accepting community. The earliest stages of growth are not about what children know, but what they feel and how adults feel about them. So it is the task of every church member to show affection, kindness, welcome and warmth to children. So they get welcomed as they arrive, for example, not just ignored while their parents get a handshake and several books. They don't get glared at or asked to leave if they make the inevitable kind of noises (or smells) which very young children do make from time to time. They do get times in the service when they can contribute in their own inimitable way, and even times when the whole thing is geared directly to them, even if it is in the crèche rather than the church. This welcoming attitude is one which children will pick up, but parents will do so even more, and a church which knows how to make children of all ages feel valued is onto a winning formula for growth.

As toddlers grow into children and then into teenagers, the acceptance of the church community becomes progressively more important. Part of growing up, as we have seen, is the need to kick against all the rules which have proscribed their life until now, to see which ones shift. It is not only parents, but churches as well, which have to develop the unyielding attitude to the truth which can absorb anger and hatred and respond with firmness and love. This can continue long past adolescence, and many a church council will have an 'angry young man' or woman among its number. This can be very healthy for the church if it means that some of its sacred cows are threatened with slaughter, but there will be many cases where youth will have to bow to experience, and youngsters have a right to learn this lesson, which will serve them well in later life. A church community which can deal with the questioning and even hostility of its younger members and respond with the same accepting love which it is showing its babies is a healthy organisation indeed.

Another problem can be the fact that youngsters will realise sooner or later that your church does not have a monopoly on truth, nor is it the only viable option for them, and they may begin to experiment with visits elsewhere. A church must accept this without taking it personally, but at the same time it must work to protect them from wandering outside the parameters of orthodox faith. This is a delicate matter, and a wise church leadership will both appreciate its own limitations and also know where the outside boundaries are. There is a lot of evidence to suggest that most children of Christian parents will grow up to mature membership of a church significantly different from that their parents brought them up within, and wise leaders and parents will recognise this phenomenon when they see it and not stand in its way. But at the same time they will try to suggest to their adolescents that the Buddhist temple down the road might not be the best place to continue their Christian discipleship.

## 3. The right to be valued

We've mentioned in our vision statement the kind of quality which we believe the children in our care deserve. The toys they play with; the materials they use; the music they listen to; the adults who look after them and the environment in which they meet: all these can be good or bad, and they are worthy of the best, because the best is what their heavenly Father would want them to have. We don't of course want to fall into the materialistic trap of equating the best with the most expensive, but we do want to avoid any sense of palming the youngsters off with the leftovers no one else wants.

But there is more to this than just material things, important though they are for showing value. As children grow older and become more established in the use of spiritual gifts, they will need to be shown that the church values the contributions they can make. Depending on your style of worship, this may be more or less difficult to manage. If you regularly have people sharing 'from the floor' what they think God is saying, it may be relatively easy for children to gain a hearing. If on the other hand your worship is more heavily controlled from the front, or if your church is simply a large one, it will be far more daunting for anyone, never mind children, to speak up.

We have a large morning service, at which the children are present, but it is rare that words or pictures are shared. If they are it is often done by jotting details down and handing them to the service leader, who will then share what he or she feels appropriate. Children can be included in this if their parents or leaders can help them with the writing, but public speaking in such a daunting context is rarely heard. But we also have another service, later in the day, where specific time is given to waiting to hear God speak. We often build in 'workshop'-type sessions, where people experiment in small groups (rather along the lines of the procedure described in chapter six). There are less youngsters at this service, but the contributions of those who do come are heard and valued, and children often join in personal ministry to those who have been touched by the Spirit. So it may not be important for the children to be able to contribute spiritual gifts at every service, as long as there is one somewhere at which they can. The larger the church the harder it is to open things up to the congregation, so look for the smaller contexts and actively encourage children there.

## 4. The right to be spiritual

As children are set free to contribute in worship, it may dawn on adults that they are indeed spiritual beings, with a spirituality of their own. This should lead to new attitudes towards them. If they're in the crèche or children's group, they're not there just to be taken out of the way while the adults get on with the real serious business. They're there to meet God in a way which is appropriate for them. So we don't give them Goldilocks or Snow White to read, since they can get that anytime; we give them little books of Bible stories. We don't show them Bill-and-Ben videos for the same reason, but we do use material which has spiritual content instead. And we have leaders who see the job not just as childminding, but as praying and talking to the children in a way which communicates the love of God to them.

As they grow, their spirituality needs to be taken seriously in other ways. The worship will include them and be relevant and appropriate for them, and adults will be happy to make minor sacrifices of style and content for the sake of allowing their spirituality to be expressed. Those who lead the worship will acknowledge the presence of children, steering a course between the twin perils of ignoring them or patronising them. So, for example, they will allow more 'rustling' time when they've announced a Bible reading or piece of liturgy, they'll speak more slowly and clearly when they expect children to join in, and they'll gladly do all the thousand-and-one other things which a little imagination and the ability to put themselves in smaller-sized shoes will tell them. We put some more hints on this area in *Liturgy and Liberty*, so we won't labour the point here.[6]

## 5. The right to be disciplined

Church is not just a free-for-all, though; children have a right to a church which disciplines them. They really do need to know that obedience, for which we have already argued strongly, is expected and enforced within the church family. They need to learn that unbridled self-expression is not their divine right, especially if it interferes with the conflicting rights of others. For their own good they have to learn that it is appropriate sometimes to be quiet and sometimes to be noisy, sometimes to bounce around and sometimes to sit still. On several occasions we have invited them to shout in worship: after all, some of the liturgy demands to be shouted. Grown-ups probably won't do this naturally, but children love it, so we include it. They can also dance more easily than most adults, so we let them, without forcing anyone else to join in. But at other times they will need to learn to behave in very different ways. As long as the church provides both sorts of times, it has the right to expect appropriate behaviour at each, and it has the right to expect that parents with young children will gladly co-operate in enforcing this behaviour. We don't think churchwardens should have to remove noisy children from services, because their parents will know what is acceptable and what isn't and will do the removing themselves. The wardens can then direct them to a quiet spot where the problem can be resolved before rejoining the service.

## 6. The right to be employed

As children grow older, they have the right to expect that they will be accepted by the church family in a way which allows them to contribute something to its life. This may involve being on a 'junior stewards' rota, and helping with the practical tasks of service management. It may, as ability increases, involve taking part in a service as adults do through leading prayers or reading from the Bible. They can be invited to help with all-age talks in one way or another, or to play or sing with a choir or music group. One of the most efficient teams in our church is the overhead projector team, which is run and staffed almost entirely by the youth group. There is always someone there to operate the OHP, they are there in good time, and they do a good job; we simply never have to worry, because it always gets done. Sadly, the same can't be said of other teams which are run by adults. This isn't all the youth group do, but they do feel it's an area where they can make a significant contribution, and they do so willingly and well.

These, then, are some of the rights which God has given to youngsters and which the church must provide for them. It all comes back, in the end, to the same old controversies which we mentioned in chapter two. Just as it is possible for John to be both a father and a brother to his sons, so children are both church members with equal rights to those of adults, but also potential rather than actual adults. To pretend, as the Children's Act seems to, that they are equal to adults in every way is clearly nonsense, but it is also wrong to say that their value to God is any less than that of adults. They have a right to be treated like children; that is, trained up and nurtured so that when they become adults physically and emotionally they can do so spiritually too. This brings us onto their responsibilities.

Your church will no doubt have agreed standards of expectation on its members. In the Free Churches these may be high; they will be less so in an Anglican setting which traditionally welcomes all-comers without much being asked of them. By seeking to discern which standards will be appropriate for children, and working to enforce them, we will be building good foundations for the future.

One example of this has already been mentioned: the responsibility for reverent behaviour. This may not mean, as most adults would want to interpret it, *quiet* behaviour, but it will mean a sense of what is appropriate at different times in the service. If we let them shout and dance at one point, they should also be able to be quiet and still at another. Our children rejoin the adults during the administration of communion, and they used to come whooping and racing into the church at the most peaceful point in the liturgy. Quite naturally, some adults found this disruptive, so the leaders talked to the children about it and they have now learnt to make their entrance a bit less dramatic. Everyone is much happier about that.

Another responsibility which we teach children concerns giving. At a time when the grown-ups were being taught about this it featured on the curriculum of all the children's and youth groups. They were taught about tithing, and most of them have now joined the envelope scheme and give regularly a tenth of their pocket money, paper-round wages, or whatever. In fact, they are streets ahead of the adults: about three per cent of our church's annual income comes from children and youth, and we'd be very surprised if they received between them three per cent of the total earnings! To be honest, their contribution isn't actually that financially significant as a proportion of our total annual turnover, but it is highly significant spiritually, because we are building for the future and establishing good habits at the very time when they are the most easy to establish. If our adult members had been trained early into tithing we'd have no financial worries at all now, and we wouldn't have to supplement our income by writing books in our spare time!

So responsibility goes hand in hand with rights, and a church which is co-operating with the children's ministry in giving rights and demanding responsibilities will help to keep the fires of the Spirit burning brightly in the young lives of our children. But we must end this chapter with a cautionary note to those working with children who find the church's leadership totally unsympathetic to their direction.

In our particular partnership the children's work leader happens to be married to the vicar, so there is no conflict of vision or direction between the two. But sadly that is not always the case. It is not the place of this book to say that a church must have a particular ethos, direction or theology of children. We've simply recommended ours, but yours is a matter which is between the leadership and God.

But we would want to say this: don't lead children's work in defiance of the leadership in a direction of which they do not approve. However good it may seem, you will be doing it out of rebellion. God will not honour it long-term, and you will model to the children in your care some attitudes which are the very opposite of those brought by the Spirit. So go to your leaders, share your vision, and ask if that is OK with them. They may well be happy with it without personally wanting to go in that direction, but if they are clearly in opposition, to go ahead would be wrong. Perhaps you should find a church with whose leadership you can agree, and go and work there. That's a hard thing to say, but we do believe it needs saying.

But what of the third corner of the triangle, the family? To this we now turn in the penultimate chapter.

### Notes

1. Polly Toynbee, writing in the *Radio Times* (12-18 March 1994).
2. J. H. Westerhoff III, *Will Our Children Have Faith?* (Seabury: USA); *Bringing Up Children in the Christian Faith* (Winston Press: USA).
3. J. Fowler, *Stages of Faith* (Harper and Row: London, 1989), and *Becoming Adult, Becoming Christian* (Harper and Row: London, 1984).

4. *Children in the Way* (The National Society/Church House Publishing: London, 1988), p 38 ff.
5. *Ibid*, p 53.
6. John Leach, *Liturgy and Liberty* (MARC: Eastbourne, 1989), p 223 ff.

# CHAPTER TWELVE

# AND FOR YOUR PARENTS?

We've said that the context created by God for children to grow into the things of the Spirit is the family, but we've been a bit ambivalent about which family. You may have spotted a potential problem when you read that bit, and it's to that problem we must now turn our attention. We made the point in the previous chapter that children will really catch fire for the Lord if they are being nurtured not just in their Sunday or weeknight groups, but also within the context of the whole church and of their human families. As we move to examine the role of the family, we need to answer two main questions.

The first concerns parents who are either ignorant of or antagonistic towards your aims as children's work leaders. Put plainly, it's this: aren't we likely to run into conflict with children's parents if we as church people start to influence their offspring, and especially if we influence them in some of the strange ways we've mentioned. In other words, what are little Johnny's mum and dad going to think when he comes home one Sunday morning and tells them he's started to speak in tongues?

This question needs dealing with under several headings according to the spiritual state of the parents in question. Some may be totally outside the life of the church and have no real understanding of faith. Their child is simply there due to the evangelistic efforts of a friend. Our children's ministry puts a high value on outreach, and the children have been encouraged in all sorts of ways to pray for and invite their friends. Occasionally we run 'bring-a-friend' mornings, which the children themselves design, and with which their parents (and indeed the whole church) co-operate. To a reasonable degree this has been successful, and we do have a number of children who are there without their parents. Members of the church family who live near them have agreed to pick them up and bring them (and are using the excuse for the steady building of relationships with their parents), and they have mostly settled in well. But doesn't this create problems?

This certainly feels as if it ought to be the case, but in our experience it simply isn't. You might expect us to have had angry complaints about brainwashing, indoctrination, turning their children funny, and so on, but in fact we've had nothing of the sort. While the parents themselves seem to have no desire for a faith (or think they've already got a totally satisfactory one), they are without exception grateful for the fact that their children are being exposed to spiritual things. Some, we suspect, are actually a bit wistful and envious of their children's growing spirituality, which may well evoke for them happy memories of their own Sunday school and the halcyon days before the church let them down by becoming irrelevant. No doubt this is not true for all parents, but it is likely that the really antagonistic ones wouldn't let their children anywhere near you in the first place. The fact that children are allowed to come demonstrates a degree of openness on their parents' part.

You may be ministering, of course, in an area where children's parents have not the first idea where they are at any given time, and would take no interest at all in their spirituality. In that case use the freedom you've got to involve children as much as you can: there will be plenty of other forces out to get them, as we've said, so you might as well fight for what is right. And then you can make deliberate attempts to build bridges to and relationships with their parents.

This is potentially a very fruitful area of ministry. We were all told in the seventies that to use children to bring parents into the church was a Bad Thing to do: now the tide is turning and we're beginning to realise that contacts made through children are important. So don't be afraid of non-Christian parents and what they might say; build friendships with them instead.

A different problem may arise if the parents are Christians, but quite honestly find all this charismatic stuff weird and terrifying. Again, the secret seems to be relationship. If the parents know the leaders, or the parents of other children in the group, and find them to be fairly normal human beings, they are likely to trust them. If their children do come home with weird ideas every once in a while, an opportunity for witness and explanation is opened up. If the point is reached where parents really do feel that their children are stepping outside the boundaries of Christian orthodoxy, they may choose to withdraw them from your group and even from your church, but this is an extreme case which we've never personally encountered. It is far more common in our experience for parents to move children out of a church because it is too dull, not because it's too lively. And if the fruit of the Spirit is steadily growing in their young lives, their parents ought to be able to notice and be glad.

A third category of parents would contain those who for one reason or another have never been taught about discipling their children, possibly because they have come into a living Christian faith more recently. If their children are older they may have done most of their parenting without the benefit of James Dobson's help, and in their attempts to co-operate with the Spirit now, they are in fact trying to move in a new direction. The more you teach on the Spirit, and the more you seem to require of children, the more threatened and deskilled they will feel.

The problem with people in this position is that the last place where they will want to talk about this is anywhere near you. So you do need to go out of your way to keep the communication channels open, and to set up opportunities for airing the issue. You'll need to remind them that we're all living in dysfunctional families, and that you certainly haven't got everything right yourself, but that you have discovered some things which can help. Above all, you want to give the message that it's never too late, and that God's redeeming love is always available to those who seek it. Once this relationship and understanding has been established, you can begin to share a few skills with them. Many people would testify to the effect of committed prayer for their youngsters whom they may have regarded as past redemption; you may feel able to offer to join them in regular prayer for their family.

And finally, what of the culture shock to children whose parents have a 'Damascus Road' conversion experience, causing everything to go up in the air? Especially if the new Christian parents head in the direction of super-spirituality, children can be left bewildered and resentful. They never used to pray at all, but now it's happening all over the place: before their breakfast, before they decide whether to go to the park or the swimming pool, and even, horror of horrors, in McDonalds! Christian tapes have ousted One FM from the stereo, and every Sunday morning now needs to be spent in the presence of those creeps who keep hugging one another and 'sharing'. Who can blame them for a bit of rebellion when this lot suddenly drops on them?

The message to parents here is 'go easy'. Children may take time to catch on, and the more dramatic their change in lifestyle, the longer it may take. You'll need to encourage them to win their children over, little by little, and not to be discouraged if they don't seem to be moving at the pace they'd like. They can be encouraged to talk to their children about the whole thing, to be honest about what's happened to them and any mistakes they feel they've made in the past, and they'll need as well to do lots of listening to understand what it feels like from the other side. You can't make children's friends for them, but there may be opportunities to encourage them to build relationships with other children from the church if to do so would seem natural and not another bit of pushing. But in the end it comes back again to the fruit of the Spirit; if God is truly at work in the parents, the children will recognise that fact because they'll become better parents.

The second question we're wanting to answer in this chapter is a much more positive one: how can parents who are fully in sympathy with what it is you're trying to do, and want to co-operate as much as they can, work with you and the church to see their children growing in the Spirit? It may not come naturally to them, so we'd like to address them now and to give them four practical pieces of advice.

## 1. Take an interest

It is very easy for children's work leaders to feel isolated from parents. If you have, and communicate, the attitudes we've mentioned about regarding them as mere baby-sitters while you worship, you'll be severely undervaluing them (unless of course that is how they regard themselves). So you'll need to take positive steps to show that you care what they're doing with your children each week.

You can do this, first of all, simply by asking: How's it going?

How is my little Johnny fitting in? Is he happy? Add to this a bit of telling: He really enjoyed that session a few weeks ago on Leviticus. Do you know what he said when he got in? And that evening in his prayers he spoke to God in a way which proved he'd really understood about the mildew regulations. He loves the model too – it's right by the side of his bed. This needn't all be crawly either: Could you explain again what you were doing last week about Infectious Skin Diseases? I don't think he quite caught it. In the context of relationship (there's that word again), this kind of conversation can help to mould you together as a team concerned with Johnny's spiritual welfare.

You could ask to visit one Sunday. Some groups will build this in anyway with a parent-helper's rota, but others ought to welcome the interest you'll bring, as long as you go in with the right attitude (we'll talk about this next). If you do visit, don't communicate the feeling that it's a great sacrifice really, and you'd much rather be in church. Do all you can to build up and encourage those who regularly miss out on teaching because they place your children higher on their list of priorities than they do themselves.

You may like to take this even further by inviting your children's ministry leader to your homegroup, Mothers' Union meeting or whatever to tell you about their vision and what they do week by week. And while you're at it, ask about the pains and frustrations of the job – you'll be surprised how many there are. Talk about how you can support one another in your different areas of ministry, and keep children's work on your prayer list – it's a front-line ministry and needs all the power and protection it can get.

And leaders, too, have a responsibility here. It is vitally important that you remain open about what it is you're doing. If you are seeking to allow the Spirit to move among the children with his supernatural power you may feel the whole thing to be a little risqué, especially if the church as a whole is less than happy about it and you are in a pioneering position. The tendency to get a bit masonic about it, and keep the details of what you do behind locked doors to the initiates only, must be resisted at all cost.

So how about an occasional meeting between children's work leaders and parents where you set out clearly your vision for the ministry and invite comments, questions and co-operation? However pioneering you may feel your work to be, most parents will probably be working with a much more traditional view of what they think you're doing. At best they may regard you as purveyors of Bible stories, and at worst they may simply be grateful to you for looking after their kids while they get on with their worship and teaching. This needs challenging, their imaginations need stretching, and they may not turn out to be anywhere near as suspicious as you might expect. When Chris was given a slot at a whole-church prayer meeting simply to explain her vision, as set out in chapter four, she was greeted with a standing ovation from the church as a whole. They had little idea as to the excitement and revolutionary nature of what she had been doing: they knew their children loved going, but that was about it. Hearing in detail not just about what was going on, but why it was going on, enabled them to buy into and rejoice in the things God was doing among them. The whole profile of the children's ministry in the church was raised significantly. So keep the lines of communication open, in both directions.

## 2. Recognise the partnership

Those who are both parents and teachers will understand something of the tension this can cause. At school they may sometimes feel (although of course never be so unprofessional as to say) that some parents who try to help, for example with reading, have no idea what they're trying to do, and cause more problems than they solve. But at home they may hear about how their little Sally has been treated at school and exclaim, 'But they don't *know* her as I do!' Here lies an issue, which can appear sometimes in the church's ministry to children. Where there is tension between parents and leaders, it can be not because of what each does know, but because of what they don't.

So leaders need to understand that they have Sally for perhaps an hour each week, while her parents have her for the rest. However much they think they understand, they simply can't know her as well as her own family do. Parents, on the other hand, need to appreciate that the children's team are doing that job because they have been called to and anointed for it by God, and recognised by the church as having at least some of the skills required. So while they may not know Sally as well as you do, they may well know more than you about how to teach and lead children into discipleship. They're not perfect, of course, any more than your parenting is perfect, but they do basically know what they're doing.

Because we have had to move around, our boys have changed schools, and the contrast between the openness and welcome to parents in the People's Republic of South Yorkshire and other schools elsewhere was striking. In Sheffield we were allowed in the building, we could even sit in on lessons if we wanted to; we looked on the teachers as our friends, and neither party felt threatened by the other's role in the care of the children. By contrast, we have been given the message elsewhere that we were not welcome any further in than the school gates, and that the staff were perfectly competent thank you very much, and would do a much better job without our interference. For children's leaders to foster relationships and co-operation will be a very large plus.

There is the potential here for great co-operation, as long as those on each side of the equation know their own roles, strengths and weaknesses, and those of the other side. So it won't simply be a case of handing your offspring over for an hour a week; rather, you'll work in partnership at providing what's best. There is also obviously the potential for great conflict as each side guards their boundaries jealously, but to take one's eyes off one's own in-securities and focus instead on the spiritual welfare of the child will help to minimise this. If you do feel uneasy, talk about it. Otherwise the Enemy will do all he can to drive a wedge between you.

## 3. Learn the skills

If your family life is not backing up the work of the children's ministry and giving children the same experiences, a tension will be set up. So parents need to be heading in the same direction, and learning to minister to their children in the same ways. Reread chapters five to eight, and ask yourself how much of this material is put into practice in your own family prayer times. Are there healings, like the one we mentioned earlier? Is there an expectation that God will speak prophetically through words or pictures as you pray together? In the final chapter we'll be making the point that adolescence is the great testing time when all that children have learnt will go through the fire of reality-testing to see if it will pass the ultimate examination, 'Does this work?' If the Spirit is active in supernatural ways in our families, the reality is established. If your children's work involves the use of the spiritual gifts, you as parents will need to begin to acquire some of the same skills so that they can be integrated into family life.

The same goes for the Bible. We needn't labour this point again here, because we've tried to make it a constant theme throughout the book. But it is a knowledge of the Scriptures which will ensure a correct use of the Spirit's gifts and encourage the growth of his fruit. It isn't enough just to buy some Bible reading-notes for them, any more than just buying them a toothbrush guarantees dental health. They'll need you there beside them to help them do it and sometimes to make them do it. We've suggested some ideas for this in *Liturgy and Liberty*, so we won't repeat them here.[1]

We said above that it's the leaders who bring a knowledge of the Spirit and the Bible to your children, but that doesn't mean that parents get let off the hook entirely. That would be as wrong as telling the leaders that they needn't bother to get to know the children, because the parents do that bit! There needs to be a partnership, but the overlap must be constantly growing.

## 4. Be worship leaders

This chapter is being written during Holy Week, and last Sunday we read in Matthew chapter 21 about the children who joined in the worship of Jesus as he rode triumphantly into Jerusalem. A great crowd of people were following him, and it is interesting to compare their worship (Mt 21:9) with that of the children (Mt 21:15). Notice anything? It's the same. Children are great imitators: what they see adults doing, they do. A little girl nurses her doll, dresses and changes it. How? In the same way she has seen her mum do it to her baby brother. A car is fitted with a little plastic stick-on steering-wheel for the kids in the back seat, and they copy the driver's every move. This is one of the main ways children learn, and in this passage it is the way they learn worship. Now here's a terrible question to have to answer: if the children in your church imitated the way their parents worship, what would they do? In fact, there's no 'if' about it: they will. Parents need to learn how to lead their children in worship, both at home and in church, and again there's some material on how to do this in John's book.

But there is one model which is very helpful for parents, but which is very commonly neglected. If your church is the sort which has someone who is called a 'worship leader', or if you've ever seen them in action at Spring Harvest or a similar event, think for a moment about what it is they do or, more particularly, what they don't do. Their job is to facilitate the worship of the congregation, but this is a highly sacrificial role. They cannot, for example, get too involved in what is going on. They can't get spaced out in wonder, love and praise when they should be getting ready for the next song. They can't just be directors, of course, while remaining totally uninvolved, because as we've said you can't lead from behind. But neither can they enter fully and personally into God's presence themselves, because they have to have one eye all the time on the congregation, so that they can meet their needs.

So they'll say things between songs, which will encourage people or focus their worship. Sometimes they'll emphasise particular lines and apply them. And on a more mundane level they'll have practical tasks too, like telling people where to find the next song or paragraph of liturgy, when to sit or stand, and so on. Those who lead worship generally manage to enjoy it and meet God through it, but it is a sacrificial rather than a selfish task.

What's that got to do with children? The fact is that if they are in church with their parents, they need their own personal worship leaders, and mum and dad are the people to do it. It is sad to look around some churches and see lots of adults in rapt states of worship while their children are busy eating hymnbooks, sicking them up again over their little sisters, playing noughts and crosses or, even worse, simply sitting there bored out of their minds. No one has bothered to lead them anywhere.

Our conviction is that parents who come to church with their children have the same role as the worship leader at the front. At times they will be whispering to their youngsters, telling them which page they're on and, even better, pointing to the words as we go through them. As the leader at the front may occasionally exhort us to 'lift our voices together' as an encouragement in worship, so mum may whisper to little Billy to 'sing up'. When the leader tells us all to keep a few moments' silence to enjoy God's presence among us, dad can echo this to Billy, enforcing it if necessary!

You see, there is a fallacy around this area: freedom is not necessarily a good thing. If we have the freedom to worship or not, there are times when we'll choose not to, because it requires less effort to sit there in a stupor. But when a leader encourages us, we make the effort and find that it was very well worth it, since we've encountered God in a way which just wouldn't have happened unless we'd been told to put some work in. The same is true with children: they won't naturally join in with worship in church, particularly if it is intended for a wider age-range than just theirs. But by cutting down their other options and helping them to do the task in hand, parents are actually setting them free to worship – free, that is, from the other things they'd rather do but which would do them less good. Parents do this all the time, for example whenever we make them eat salad rather than just chips, so why baulk at doing it in worship?

But it does need to be understood that this is a sacrificial ministry, and parents need to recognise that they will only have one eye available for God if the other is to be kept on Billy. That's why it's important that at times they worship without him being present (Billy, not God), either because he's out with the children's group or because he's at home for the evening with a baby-sitter. But to get on with it yourself while leaving him to his own devices will do nothing to help him grow in the Spirit. In fact, the opposite may be true: his boredom may lead to disenchantment.

So there are some hints for parents about working together with the children's ministry and the church as a whole. 'A cord of three strands is not quickly broken,' said the Teacher (Eccl 4:12). By tying together these different influences on children, the work of the Spirit in them will be enabled and enhanced. A strong foundation for the future will be built, and that future will be met with an abiding faith in Jesus. For the final chapter we'll take a look into that future and see what might change as our children grow up.

## Notes

1. John Leach, *Liturgy and Liberty* (MARC: Eastbourne, 1989), p 223 ff.

# CHAPTER THIRTEEN

# GROWING UP

So far most of what we've said has been mainly applicable to younger children, and you may perhaps have found this a bit of a frustration. If your children, or the children you work with, have moved on into adolescence, you may have read so far with a sense of wistfulness and nostalgia for the days when it was as easy as that. But now it's different, and a whole new set of rules seem to apply. Is there anything which can be helpful to those working with older children and teenagers?

At one level the simple answer is 'no'. This is not a book about youth work, and it has never purported to be. Neither can we claim any real experience with teenagers, although of course like most curates and wives we've done our stint with the church youth group. But we did so without much in the way of enthusiasm or flair, and we've never considered it our calling. What's more, our own children have so far escaped the traumas of adolescence, although the writing is currently on the wall with one of them! So we really can't say a lot which will be credible for those who know from first hand the dangers, toils and snares of that particular age-group.

But there may paradoxically be some advantages to this. Our lack of experience does give us a certain naive objectivity, and the thinking we have done about children can, we feel, be extrapolated a bit further. We do have some things to say which we believe to be true, and we can believe them because hard experience has not yet proved us wrong. And of course, like everyone else with eyes and ears, we have been able to observe some of the things going on around us, and some of the mistakes we see being made. And when we look back, that is how we learnt quite a bit about what we know about children.

We got married rather later than most of our peers, and then waited a further five years before Steve was born. So while we were in the blissful state of freedom, many of our friends were well into babies, toddlers and even fully-fledged children. We never studied parenting to any great degree at that stage, but we were often to be heard remarking, 'When *we* have kids they won't behave like that!' It was this experience which taught us much of what we learnt, and which we seek to practise today. Our friends, had they overheard us, could well have given us knowing looks which said, 'You wait!' We knew nothing, we had no experience of what it was like to cope with two-year-olds' tantrums or any of the other horrors which formed their daily diet. And yet the objectivity we did have enabled us to set out principles which subsequently proved to be successful (in as far as our parenting can be judged to be successful, which mercifully most of our readers will never know!).

In the same way, therefore, we believe we do have some things to say about adolescence, not from our experience of practicalities, but from our thinking about principles.

First of all, we would want to question the tacit assumption that our children will turn rebellious and nasty when their hormones get going at about thirteen. There seems to be a resignation and terror in many if not most parents that they are in for several years of hell which will end up with their children totally rejecting all they have been taught for the first dozen years of their life. We believe, naively perhaps, that *it needn't be like that*. Job, in the midst of his pain and suffering, exclaimed, 'What I feared has come upon me; what I dreaded has happened to me' (Job 3:25). Those experienced in the world of counselling would point to this verse as a key one for understanding pain and fear: it's almost as if we will trouble onto ourselves if we worry about it too much.

Many parents, including, amazingly, many Christian parents, have bought what we believe to be a lie, and when it does work out as they feared and expected, they shrug their shoulders and say, 'I told you so!' The Bible, which is never afraid to give warnings when difficult times lie ahead, says nothing about the need for adolescence to be a tragedy. Our whole culture has been cursed with this expectation, and the more it does happen, the more we believe the curse. We firmly reject this, and we're holding on to the hope that however taxing the adolescent years may be, they won't *necessarily* be disastrous. They may be, of course – nobody is denying that – but we will simply not accept the inevitability of it. We're not under the control of the teenage years: we have some control over them. Whether or not they prove to be one long tragedy will be affected to a high degree by the way we handle them.

This ought to be good news for parents approaching this phase, but it also lays a big responsibility on them, and it may lay a great deal of guilt on those who feel they have failed in some way. If it's true, they can't just blame hormones; they could themselves have helped things to be different. Now, our desire is not in any way to load guilt on people, but a true understanding of the situation is a good place to start in the work of redemption, for which, as we've mentioned, there is plenty of grace with God. So what is going on in adolescence, and how can we help it to pass with as little trauma as possible?

First, there are of course physical changes taking place. Hormones do cause temper tantrums, mood swings, sudden fluctuations when our little baby becomes a loutish oaf and vice versa. That is a biochemical fact, and the Spirit's power is not given to bypass this process. And there are psychological changes too, with the growing distance between parents and children, an increasing need to question and test the assumptions which they've lived with all their lives, and the traumatic realisation that dad and mum are not the supermen and women their children had believed them to be. All this was built into us by our creator God as part of the process of letting go, and it is basically a good and necessary process. The question is: where is the dividing line between that which God has created good, and that which through sin the Enemy has spoiled? Where can we expect the sanctifying work of the Spirit to make a difference, and where musn't we expect him to bypass the important but painful work of separation into adulthood?

It's not only family relationships which can be affected by adolescence. Statistics have shown that the teenage years are the stage where the greatest number of people lose their contact with the church and their faith (and, conversely, where the greatest number find faith). Many Christian parents are saddened by their teenagers' rebellion against them, but even more so by their rebellion against God. Traditional Sunday-school methods have quite simply failed to hold on to children successfully. When we were confronted in 1991 with the statistics about church decline from 1979 to 1989, we were told that forty per cent of the 1,000 people who stopped going to church each week of those ten years were under fifteen, and eighty-seven per cent under thirty.[1] Even in some of the denominations which are experiencing net growth, there is still decline among the child membership.[2] All in all, we have no evidence whatsoever to suggest that the way we've been doing children's ministry in the past has worked. Is there any hope that the greater exposure to the Spirit which this book argues for will make any significant difference? The only answer to that is 'time will tell', but it is our conviction that the work of the Spirit ought to make adolescence less traumatic, if not totally trauma-free.

Let's begin to answer some questions, first of all by asking another one, and then by looking at a case-study. The all-important question is, 'What are adolescents searching for?' If we can understand that, we might be able to see how we can help them find it.

## Stability

So much is changing, in teenagers' bodies, their minds and their circumstances, that they can end up confused and angry. Anything which can bring stability into this bubbling cauldron of uncertainty will do a tremendous amount of good. They probably won't be able to articulate their need for it, and they may kick very hard against it (of which more later), but they desperately need it. Those whose parents have split up during this period, for example, will speak eloquently of the added pain this caused at an already difficult time. On the other hand, those whose home and church life is stable will be able to see, even if only in retrospect, the value it was to them.

Recently a little boy in our congregation was very ill, and spent a long time in intensive care. It really was unclear whether or not he would pull through, but eventually he did, and returned home, amidst great rejoicing in the church family. But he was different. He would go into fits of uncontrollable temper, or sobbing, or all kinds of other antisocial behaviour. His parents, while grateful for his recovery, were filled with anxiety about him. They knew from their experience of counselling that severe traumas can sometimes allow access to demonic forces, and John was called in to pray with the boy. While believing in the possibility of such oppression, he found it hard to imagine how someone who had been so soaked in prayer throughout the illness could have fallen prey to the Enemy in this way, so he phoned a friend who was both spiritually experienced and a doctor working with children. Was it common, he asked, for children to be disturbed in this way? The answer he got contained a profound message which is equally applicable to adolescence: if someone begins suddenly to behave differently, it is usually because they have been treated differently. And so it was. For weeks little Simon had been the centre of attention: he could eat, or leave, what he felt like and sleep or wake when he felt like it; his crying was immediately treated with sympathy and comfort; there were people around to cater for his every need, instantly, and finally his grateful parents, so relieved to have him safely back, indulged him with all sorts of treats and fed him up to help him regain the weight he'd lost. John did go and pray, but it was when the parents began to treat him consistently again, and to re-establish the behaviour-boundaries which had previously been enforced, that his tantrums began to subside and he made a full recovery.

When the adolescent tantrums first appear, it is very tempting for parents suddenly to throw all the rules out of the window as if a terminal illness had set in. When a teenager needs stability more than ever, this is a big mistake. So we intend to make sure that we keep up the family standards of behaviour which we've always expected. Our children should, as it were, be able to sing to parents and to churches, as well as to God, 'O Thou who changest not, abide with me' when all around (and within) is change and decay.

## Independence

Secondly, adolescence is about the search for independence, becoming a person in one's own right, and not just an extension of one's parents. Painful though this is for both parties, it must happen. The first time they go out on their bikes alone; the first day at secondary school; the first Scout or Guide camp; the new motorbike; even the first time they sit with someone else in church: all these are great traumas for parents, but vitally important for the kids. Parents may be left feeling obsolete and superfluous, and that hurts after one has given the best years of one's life to someone else. They may resent rather than welcome the growing relationships with other adult role-models, such as youth leaders, which it is so important for them to develop. They may even feel envious of the opportunities which young people have nowadays which they simply didn't have when they were young, and this envy may lead them into a subconscious limiting of their children's experiences.

Then, of course, there's the danger. The fear of parents is that once our offspring are out of our control, all manner of disasters too terrible to articulate will befall them. And of course, it has to be said, they might. That's why it's so frightening. The art is to know when to allow and when to forbid such activities, and to know why.

This independence is not just about physical separation; it is about intellectual distancing too. Values we've taught need to be examined and often rejected, at least for a while. This may show itself in dress style and behaviour patterns. There is almost the desire to shock for its own sake, but also a burning need to fit in with the peer group. John spent most of the late sixties trying to sneak out of the door with his mum's fur coat on inside-out (he couldn't afford a real Afghan) before his dad caught him and told him he wasn't going out looking like that. The battle continues, and wise parents will realise it has nothing to do with clothing but everything to do with independence. Parents who are secure in their relationship with their teenagers can save themselves considerable pain by a deliberate choice of which battles to fight and which to choose to lose. If every little thing becomes a major issue with bad feelings around twenty-four hours a day, life can get very uncomfortable. So why not choose the important battles to fight, and let them have a funny hairstyle if they want?

The same issues apply on a spiritual level. We've already said that many children are unlikely to find a spiritual home in the same church or tradition as their parents, but the anxiety caused by their first trip to the house-church down the road can be every bit as great as any of the above forays, and the perceived dangers just as great. Thus we react with fear and possibly anger. To cultivate a trust that they are in God's hands, and to rejoice that they are healthy enough to begin to venture out, is difficult indeed. But the more we try to stop them, the harder they'll try to go. Why?

Because God has built into them the need to go, and rightly so.

The kind of discipling we do with young children can affect deeply this quest for spiritual independence. If we teach them, directly or by implication, that *our* church is the only real one, the struggle to find a spiritual home later will be that much harder. But if we build in an understanding that in all the different tribes there are those who are God's people, and even that they may well one day want to move to a different tribe, the move if it comes will be much smoother. Some churches seem more interested in building an empire than in building the kingdom: children will pick this up, and it'll provide one more thing for them to kick against later. But if we set bigger boundaries within which they can explore and find their place, the whole exercise will be that much less painful.

## Experience

The teenage years form a time when new experiences await them at every turn. Part of the nature of adolescence is a desire to explore them to the full. Sex and drugs and rock-and-roll are out there to be discovered, and whether it is their first Benson and Hedges or their first charismatic service, there is a thrill in the new, a thrill enhanced if the new is also slightly naughty. Again, this can be a threatening time for parents, very aware of the dangers but totally oblivious to the fact that they did exactly the same things themselves and are still here to tell the tale. (Or, alternatively, it may be that they remember only too well their own experiences, and want to protect the next generation from the mistakes they made!) This is often where the crunch comes with church: Bible stories may have been fine up to this point, but lots more is needed if they are to stick around.

## Reality

Along with this comes a testing-out of all that they once held dear. In particular, this holds true spiritually. All the things they've been brought up to believe and value are interrogated with one big question, 'Does this work?' If they've been brought up with Christian values and Bible stories, they'll want to know, and to prove by experience, that the whole deal passes this test. And this, it has to be said, is where the church has fallen down with the hardest bump. The things they learnt in Sunday school, but which were never applied, are simply irrelevant. The experiences of people in the Bible whom they read about without ever experiencing the same things themselves are just so many fairy tales. We've explained before our conviction that knowledge and experience must go in partnership, because in the teenage years knowledge is almost equated with experience. A teenager who has only *heard* from the Bible about healing or speaking in tongues (and even they are sadly few) will stand less chance of surviving adolescence spiritually intact than one who has healed or spoken in tongues. Children's work leaders have taught, parents have backed up the teaching, the church has made space for him to minister, and his own experience is still with him: that's reality. There are no double standards or hypocrisy or hollowness (all of which youngsters can sniff out a mile away), and nothing to suggest that this needs questioning. It works!

## Purpose

The teenage years are those during which a new, personal identity must be found. Particularly within the church family, there is a need to make a mark and find a niche. It is an idealistic time, with high hopes and high principles abounding. Our world and its Prince, threatened by the potential power of this idealism if God was ever to get his hands on it, have managed to divert it onto safer issues like rainforests and baby seals, but if our children's ministry has taught children to dream dreams for God instead, there is tremendous power waiting to be unleashed.

Some children feel quite early a calling from God on their lives. This must of course be tested and refined: our Paul decided strongly for one period of his life that he wanted to be a milkman; it took some time before we twigged that this calling appeared at a phase when we were constantly sending him back to bed in the morning because he was getting up too early. The thought of being on the road by five am *legally* was captivating for him! But now he knows he's been gifted as an evangelist; he doesn't mind who he tells (including his RE teacher at school), and he is already showing success in this field by witnessing to friends and bringing them to church with him. If the church and families don't take this growing need for a calling and purpose seriously, and help them to see that souls are more important than deodorants and saving milk-bottle tops, teenagers will be beset by self-doubt and find fulfilment elsewhere. The good can indeed be the enemy of the best.

## Security

But there is one thing above all which teenagers require during these difficult years: security. One youth worker has told us that the thing which really touches street-wise teenagers is to see people who are committed to them. In all sorts of ways they need to kick against the boundaries which they will perceive to have been hedging them in until now, but they need to know that there are some boundaries which will not move. They need to be sure of their parents' love and the acceptance of the church family. It's almost as if some of them will go out of their way to test it: You say you love me? Well love me after *this*! Rules are disobeyed; rooms are left untidy (no change there from childhood); rudeness and arguments follow one after the other: Now love me! comes the challenge. But if we don't, their whole world crashes in. It's a bit like when you come downstairs in the dark and think you've reached the ground, only to find you've miscounted. Suddenly there's nothing there to put your foot on, and it's all you can do to stop yourself from tumbling headlong. Prove you love me, and prove your stupid rules still apply: that's the challenge.

If these are some of the things teenagers are searching for during adolescence, can the Spirit help them, and parents, and churches to provide them? Let's look at a case-study to end this chapter, and let's use one particular family in whom the Spirit lived more fully than any other. It'll be an interesting study, because it'll help us to see how things should be, since the Spirit lived in one member of the family totally and completely, but it'll also show us reality, because the other members, like us, are not perfect. The incident in question is recorded for us in Luke's Gospel chapter 2.

Jesus is twelve, not a bad age for an adolescent. He's with his family, doing what they always do (Lk 2:42). There's the *stability*. The adolescents in many of our families would be lying with the covers pulled up over their heads saying, 'Mum do I *have* to go to the Temple this year?' Whether or not this conversation took place, he went.

Then there's the *independence* (Lk 2:43-44). He's in the crowd, they think, but he'll be OK; he's big enough to be trusted without wearing his reins any longer. For a whole day he's on his own, and isn't even missed. The problem is that he's not in the crowd at all; he's out looking for *experience* (Lk 2:46). Maybe he's already felt the call of his Father on his life to be a rabbi and a teacher, so he wants to see how it feels to be with some.

He's also searching for *reality*. There's a discussion going on. He's been rooted and grounded in the Scriptures, but he wants to know more. It would be fascinating to know what he was talking to the teachers about, but sadly we're not told. But clearly he wants to know, and he's wanted to know for three solid days.

His parents arrive and he gets a telling-off, not totally unjustified, we may feel. But his answer shows that he's found *purpose* (Lk 2:49). He's now got a higher purpose in life; his Father, rather than his parents, is now calling the shots. But note finally the *security* he finds (Lk 2:51) as he remains obedient to his earthly parents and returns to normal family life, as far as we know for the next eighteen years. The outcome? 'Jesus grew in wisdom and stature, and in favour with God and men' (Lk 2:52).

We've looked at this story from Jesus' point of view: what about his parents? Look at the emotions involved, and see if they ring any bells for you. The anxiety, first of all, as they discover he's missing, and the terrified searching which lasts for three days. The relief at finding him which shows itself in anger. The exasperated cry of, 'Why have you treated us like this?' and the total incomprehension of his answer to them. All these are experiences which every parent either has known or will know.

So what can we learn, both from the perfection of Jesus and the real-life reactions of Mary and Joseph? How can we see the work of the Spirit making a difference, and how can we hope to survive the teenage years more or less intact?

Note, first of all, the politeness of Jesus and his obedience. He doesn't throw a wobbly when his parents tell him off; he doesn't shout at them or argue with them; rather he obeys them. The fruit of the Spirit, which has been growing in him for twelve years, is

manifested in his even temper, and his desire to explain rather than
argue, even when his parents haven't got the foggiest what he's on
about. There is explanation rather than resentment, and
communication instead of withdrawal and the sulks. This speaks
well of the foundations laid in his heart by his parents and the Spirit
working together: it is for this that we argued in the earlier chapters
of this book. Our teenagers may get angry with us, and vice versa,
but none of us need respond in the ways which Paul calls 'the acts
of the sinful nature' in Galatians 5:19 if we have all grown the fruit
of the Spirit which he goes on to list (Gal 5:22-23).

Another important principle appears in verse 49 with Jesus'
words, 'Didn't you know . . .?' This shouldn't have taken you by
surprise, he's saying. Neither should our children's adolescence
take us by surprise. With a bit of imagination we can predict the
likely issues which will arise, and we can prepare for them. We
don't believe it to be inevitable that one of our boys will announce
to us one day that he is moving in with his girlfriend, but neither
will we be surprised if he does: we've got our answer ready. This
proactive style of parenting means that we won't need to be
reactive; in other words we won't respond out of shock or anger,
and say things which we'll later regret. All sorts of likely issues
have already been faced in our imagination, and we feel as
prepared as we can for them. It's not that we'll never be shocked or
angry or hurt – we haven't got *that* much imagination, but we hope
we won't go careering through the teenage years tossed about by
totally unforeseen waves of fortune. For the sake of the boys'
security we need to retain a degree of control, and forewarned is
indeed forearmed. If you're reading this chapter before the great
and terrible day of the twelfth birthday, you can do things now to
prepare. It'll save lots of wasted rage later.

It's not just parents who can be proactive. As they approach
adolescence, our children are approaching a time of great
turbulence. It needn't be nasty, and we can tell them that as well as
believing it ourselves, but it will be strange. We have found it very
helpful to begin working with Steve through a book called
*Preparing for Adolescence*[3] which helps young teenagers to get
ready for some of the things they'll experience over the next few
years. Even if it doesn't help the actual process, it can certainly
take some of the shock away, and it has opened up all sorts of

subjects for discussion. The talks themselves are helpful, but even more so is the lesson that we *can* talk about things like this.

Trust in God's faithfulness is another quality which the Spirit brings to us. Parents may need this a lot more than their children do, and it won't make us totally immune from anxiety, but ultimately all things work together for good if we're God's people. Of course we'll worry, but we can model to our children a simple trust which will be a great stabilising influence on them during the tumultuous years they go through.

Note as well that discipline never breaks down in this story. At the start and at the end Jesus is subject to his parents. The boundaries may have been strained a little, but they haven't moved. Jesus' parents have made it possible for him to obey both his earthly (Lk 2:48) and his heavenly (Lk 2:49) fathers. So often we set up false dichotomies, even as Christian parents. If the worst bit of rebellion your children come up with is that they want to change to the Pentecostal church you're fortunate indeed. Don't make a big issue of it; thank God that they still want to go somewhere. Thousands don't!

The big issue here is serving God. Jesus' heart is set on that, even if it isn't in quite the way his parents (or his home synagogue) were expecting. It is sad when churches stifle attempts by teenagers to do something significant for God because it doesn't fit the style or ethos of the church. And it is wonderful when the leadership can see the desire there and make space for it. It may need refining, but then so do most of our ideas, if we're honest. Bill Hybels runs the largest church in America, the famous Willow Creek Community Church near Chicago. It began when he formed a partnership with a musician called Dave Holmbo and began to run Bible studies attached to music rehearsals. From a youth group of twenty-five, he now leads a church with a Sunday attendance of 15,000 people. Yet many times along the way things could have been threatened by the church authorities.[4] So it may be that among the crazy ideas your youth groups come up with, there is a real winner. How sad to miss out on it, and how rejecting for those behind it. It's as if Mary got Jesus home, smacked him round the ear and said, 'That's the last time I let you out of my sight!' If only our churches could learn to treasure the things our youngsters are trying to teach us. In our experience it is those churches which have opened their life consciously to the wind of the Spirit which are more happy to take risks, and which are more likely to expect to hear him speaking in unexpected ways, even sometimes through teenagers!

This hasn't been the last word on adolescence, but we have attempted to show how the Spirit can help. The writer of Proverbs (whoever he was!) wrote these words: 'Train a child in the way he should go, and when he is old he will not turn from it' (Prov 22:6). The principle here is that what we do with children will affect how they turn out as adults. It's no good waiting; it could be too late by then.

We very much hope that this book has given you some practical hints about how this training up might be achieved in partnership with the Holy Spirit, whom the Father gives so that we might be holy and Christ-like. There's no money-back guarantee; after all, it is people we're dealing with, and they're all different and special. But they're all special to God too, and we wouldn't want them to miss out on anything he might have for them. The promise of the Spirit is for us who believe and for our children; let's do all we can to help them receive that most precious gift.

## Notes

1. P. Brierley, *'Christian' England* (MARC Europe: London, 1991), p 82 f.
2. *Ibid*, p 51 ff.
3. James Dobson, *Preparing for Adolescence* (Kingsway: Eastbourne, 1982).
4. You can read the Willow Creek story in Martin Robinson's *A World Apart* (Monarch: Tunbridge Wells, 1992).